FROM DARKNESS
TO LIGHT

Fiona Lynch

To Tom + Doddie

Thankyou for your contributions to The Church of United Nations.

God bless you

Fiona

25. 7. 10

Published by Lulu.com 2008

Copyright © 2008 Fiona Lynch, 'From Darkness to Light.'

All rights reserved. Any unauthorised broadcasting, public performance, copying will constitute an infringement of copyright.

ISBN 978-1-4092-1218-8

All names have been changed to protect identity.

DEDICATION

I dedicate this book to my six children.

May they walk in the light.

ACKNOWLEDGEMENTS

I would like to express great gratitude and thanks to Andrew Chamberlain, and to Bill Brown for their sincere guidance and direction in the production of this book. I would like to give a special thank you to Ivan John, and his wife for their great support to me at a time when I was in desperate need. And to my children who have been patient with me in writing this book. Thank you all.

CONTENTS

Part one – The Darkness   Page

Introduction   8
Chapter 1 – The formation of my life   9
Chapter 2 – The Unexpected Trap   24
Chapter 3 – The Pain Goes Deeper   31
Chapter 4 – When the Seed Was Sown   48
Chapter 5 – Violence and Control   60
Chapter 6 – When Enough's Enough   79
Chapter 7 – Walking towards Darkness   95
Chapter 8 – Looking for answers   111
Chapter 9 – The Pipe!   128
Chapter 10 – A Young Man's Slave   138
Chapter 11 – Directed by Dreams   153
Chapter 12 – The Darkness Continues   171
Chapter 13 – My Support   184
Chapter 14 – A Glimmer of Hope   194

Part Two – The Light   **Page**

Chapter 15 – The Mystery Trail Begins   207

Chapter 16 – The Man in my Dream   219

Chapter 17 – The Spiritual Dimension   240

Chapter 18 – Disillusioned   263

Chapter 19 – Searching for the Truth   274

Chapter 20 – Finding the Truth   290

Epilogue – The Hidden Treasures   301

PART ONE

THE DARKNESS

INTRODUCTION

There are some people who become detached from society, living a life that leads to nothing. It can happen to anyone, for a variety of reasons. I know, because it happened to me. This is why I have written this book, to help those who are at a point of wanting to turn their life around, but do not know how, and for those who are looking for a new hope in life but are struggling with pains from the past. I hope this book gives encouragement, hope and joy, to all who are searching for relief, from their pains or problems, and for those who are seeking answers in life.

CHAPTER 1

THE FORMATION OF MY LIFE

I was born one of five children in England, in a place called Cambridge. My sisters, Andrea, Janet, my twin Natasha, and my little sister Mirianne, lived with our parents in a small three bed roomed semi-detached house. My mum and dad had us close together. Five children, all under the age of five, so we were all friends, as well as sisters.

Natasha and I had a very special relationship. We were identical twins, although she was slightly bigger than me. We always wore the same clothes and everyone would get us mixed up. It was so funny!

"You're, err, Natasha," people would guess to me.

"You're, err, Fiona," they would guess to Natasha.

They would always get it wrong. But we got used to it.

Natasha and I always felt each other's pain, and would feel the need to protect each other. We were very secretive and would always whisper to each other to the annoyance of our other siblings.

"Look at the twins," they would say. "They're whispering again."

Natasha and I just could not help it. We loved each other, so much. She was the other half of me and I was the other half of her. So even if we fell out with each other, no one could say anything that would imply they were taking sides, otherwise we would both turn on them because we would feel hurt for the one who was accused of being in the wrong!

Although I had the protection of my twin sister, the early years of my life were very difficult. It was the belief that 'children should be seen and not heard,' which was forcefully applied.

The adult world appeared to be separate from the world of children. Abuse on children was more open physically and verbally. With the parents not realising that this was abuse! I had always believed that this was a cultural thing, until I became an adult and discovered that it occurred in most cultures.

Children spoke when they were spoken to. They always made sure they said please and thank you. If not, they would be in serious trouble. It was that kind of era. With the strict discipline I received at home and because of my colour and culture, I had difficulty knowing exactly where I fitted into the community around me.

My character was of a soft nature; very quiet and shy. I found it hard to have a conversation in front of any one. If I was spoken to, or asked a question in front of a group of people, Natasha would always speak for me. She understood my fears. I would hide behind her for security, holding onto my ear with my head leant to one side, feeling indifferent to everyone, whether they were from my culture or from the English culture. I found it hard to relate to and accept cruelty and had difficulty understanding how people could be so horrible to each other. This and my lack of confidence suppressed my personality.

I became a yes person and would never say no in case I hurt or let somebody down. Although people would tell me, no and let me down! This led to controlling by others later in my life.

I was a very thin child and stayed thin throughout most of my adulthood. This added to my feelings of inadequacy. People did not take me seriously. Because of my frail looking appearance they saw me as weak. I had a thing about food. I could not understand why people ate what I thought, was a lot, especially if they weren't hungry. As a baby my mum said she had to put solid food into a bottle and squeeze it into my mouth to make sure I ate.

As I got older I became fearful about eating in case I became too big. My mum had gained a lot of weight and had told us that she was once very slim. Although it was not mum's fault, her words had an impact on my mind and added to my thoughts about food. I would look in the mirror to see this big person although I was only seven stone. I became anorexic then bulimic. My mum would take me back and forth to the doctors. She was desperate for me to eat. I was given so many different tonics to stimulate my appetite but none of them worked. I thought I would never be like everyone else and enjoy food.

As a young girl, I was sexually molested by friends of the family. One occasion was when all the family attended a wedding. I wore a smart lilac dress my mum had made. She loved to sew and had spent the week before making dresses for me and my sisters. It had been an enjoyable day. I danced and ran around with the other children that were there. Innocent and happy.

A man asked me to sit on his lap. I did not know who he was and I couldn't see what he looked like because the lights were dimmed in the room. Because of my upbringing, I did as I was told.

I was going through puberty at the time. This man grabbed at my developing breasts. He squeezed and twisted them as tight as he could, not caring about the effect this would be having on me.

Suddenly everything seemed to go dark. I sat quietly. I was scared and in agony. All I could do was wait until this man had finished assaulting me. I looked around wondering why nobody came to help? Could they not see? Everyone was too busy having a good time, to notice what was happening to me. After sometime he finally let me go. I slid off his lap wondering if this was normal.

On other occasions when a family friend visited the house, every time he came round he would sit me and my sisters on his lap.

"Mind the snake,' he would say.

As a child I was not sure what he meant and what it was that I was feeling. However, I now realise what this snake was!

Growing up in Western Society was very difficult for me as a black child; it was pointless talking about things like hair and food with my schoolmates. I would feel embarrassed about what I ate, as they could not relate to it. They would ask me to describe Jamaican dishes and would then say "Ugh, what's that?" making me feel awkward. So I always avoided the subject.

My afro hair was completely different from their straight hair. My sisters and I always wondered what it would be like to have straight hair. We would make pretend wigs out of mum's old headscarves by cutting strands around the edges... wrapping it around our heads. We would shake our heads letting the strands fall into our eyes, to see what it was like: to be able to tuck it behind our ears. This made no difference to the way that I felt.

My parents had come to Britain from Jamaica for a chance to make a better life for themselves. Britain was in need of semi-skilled workers to help build up the introduction of the welfare system. Britain was advertising abroad for workers. Many West Indians came over and became either nurses or bus drivers, including my mum and dad.

When they arrived in England they had nothing. They worked very hard to make ends meet for me and my sisters. Mum worked night shifts at a hospital for the elderly and dad worked for Eastern Companies, bus services. He worked from the early hours of the morning to late at night. Because of this, me and my sister's had to become responsible at a very young age. My eldest sister would help mum out by washing us, doing our hair and putting us to bed.

As I became a teenager I remember more and more white people were becoming vocal on their opinions about black people. And it was all negative. The arrival of the skinheads was an example of white supremacy rearing its ugly head. Throughout my life, I have feared the skinheads as in a similar way, many white people were afraid of being confronted by a group of black people.

However, the threat of violence towards blacks by skinheads was quite evident to me. When I was about fifteen or sixteen years of age, my sisters and I were walking to a local disco. We were just about to go under a subway when a taxi pulled up which appeared to arrive from the middle of nowhere. The driver, who was white, shouted at us.

"Don't go under the sub-way," he stressed, with great urgency in his voice.

"Why?" we asked.

"There's loads of racist skinheads under there. Burning a fire and chanting; your lives will be in danger if you go down there. Get out of the area, quick!"

Hearing the sound of the singing and chanting we realised the meaning of what he was saying. Frightened for our lives, we thanked him and ran as fast as we could. Praise God, we were saved that night from something dreadful.

Because of the threat of violence and harsh immigration laws, mum and dad tried their best to keep me and my sisters under control. They were afraid of what other people would think about us. So they would not allow us to mix with other races outside of school. Most children from a working class background on the council estate we lived in, appeared to us, to be rude to their parents and would play out on the streets until late at night. Mum did not want us to be led astray, so out of school hours and during the school holidays we spent most of our social time mixing with our cousins. And on Sunday's we would go to a black Pentecostal church.

I remember when I was about six years old, having an awareness of my being and knowing there was a God. I never questioned the existence of God but I did his colour. Everyone in church was black and I became confused as to why God was white. All the pictures I saw of Jesus were white! Being black, in a predominantly white society was enough to make me feel alienated, let alone God our creator being white. Although it seemed unfair to me, I pushed this thought to the back of my mind.

My mum was very strict and was firm with her words. She stood her ground to what she believed was right, whereas my dad was quite the opposite. He was very quiet and never shouted at us. It was left to mum to discipline me and my sisters. Mum was very proud of us and worked very hard to make sure that the house was kept clean and in order, and that my sisters and I had what we needed to survive. We had daily chores to do and if we stepped out of line, we soon knew about it. Despite this, we still had many happy, and fun moments as a family.

Mum and Dad would always tell us about Jamaica and how beautiful it was and how the sun was always shinning. I would feel excited but at the same time sad, as I could not fully understand why my parents had come to a cold place like England and where the majority of people were white. Mum and dad would tell us ghost stories and how people spoke to ghosts in Jamaica as though it was normal. We would get scared and spooked out, but in a fun kind of way. We also had good times as a community, without attaching ourselves to the outside world. In the summer months, we would go to watch cricket matches. Jamaicans loved cricket and the black community had their own team. After every match was a party. As we got older the team dissolved so my dad set up another one, which lasted for several years. Dad was good at organising social activities, including days out. Because dad worked on the buses, he would hire a bus and promote day trips to the seaside or day trips to Holland and Belgium for anyone who wanted to go. This meant there was always something to do.

When I was eight years old, mum and dad got a mortgage for their own property so we moved onto a private road. The road was very different from the council estate I had always known. It was quiet and peaceful with no children running around late into the evening.

The house had three bed rooms with a large back garden. There were many fruit trees, like an orchard. There were pear trees and apple trees and black berry bushes. As children, this made us very excited about the move. I remember running down the long garden for the first time. This gave me a new sense of freedom because the house was ours. My twin sister and I shared one room, which was situated at the front of the house next to my parent's room, and my other three sisters shared the other room at the back of the house. So they had the view of the garden.

On one side of us lived a German couple who did not like the look of us and were not pleased to have us as their neighbours. They would look at us as though we were beneath them. The thought of living next to black people seemed to offend them even though they were not from England. They sold up and left.

On the other side of us lived an old woman called Mrs. Nottingham. She was seventy when we moved in and lived to be nearly a hundred years old. She lived with her husband until after the Second World War. She told us Mr. Nottingham had come home from work and had gone upstairs to have a bath. After hearing a loud bang, she went upstairs to see what it was and found her him on the floor dead. They never had children so she had no one to keep her company. The only relative was a niece who used to pop round from time to time.

Mrs. Nottingham was a lovely lady who accepted us. We used to go round to visit her. As children we found both her and her house fascinating. All her furniture was pre-war... very old fashioned! She had a small wooden child's chair that she used to treat regularly for woodworm to preserve it. She told us it was over a hundred years old. She even had an air raid shelter in her back garden which was now covered over. She would often tell us stories of the past and this gave me an insight into Victorian England and what it was like to live through the war.

Primary school for me was a very lonely time. I had a tough time trying to fit in. I could sense the racism from some of the other children. One particular girl would sneer at me whenever she had the opportunity. She was known to dislike black people. I felt intimidated by her. I was made to feel like her subject. Not knowing who to turn to for help, I had no choice but to accept it.

My twin sister was always there for me which gave me some kind of protection, but she was not always aware of how lonely I felt. When she couldn't go to school due to illness, I dreaded it. The silence for me, and inside of me was agonising.

I can remember one day at school. I was in the playground. I wore a skirt and tights with a hooded jacket. It was winter and very cold so I had the hood up. From behind no one could see my afro hair or the colour of my skin. This boy shouted, "hey, you." By the tone of his voice it sounded as if he was interested, till I turned round. He saw I was black. He looked embarrassed and ran off. I turned back round and carried on walking, head down, saddened by his response towards me.

As I progressed onto secondary school, I became interested in history. We were taught English and American history, but nothing was mentioned about slavery or the role of black men and women. It seemed that there was no history about black people and all of mankind was white! It was not until a weekly programme called 'Roots' was shown on the TV that I became aware of black people being used as slaves. The programme showed the horrendous treatment that black slaves had received. They were whipped, hung and were falsely accused of things they did not do. They would be spoken to, with no respect. It broke my heart to watch, making me feel like a second class citizen.

As I grew up people would compare me and my twin. She had always been more outgoing and confident than I was. She was perceived as being more intelligent and capable of being responsible. This got on our nerves and had a really negative effect on me. I believed I would amount to nothing so I did not take my education seriously and began to rebel. I gained popularity by playing up and doing silly things. It did not matter if I got into trouble with the teachers. I gained the attention of my class mates. I gained a kind of strength from this and I started to feel part of a team.

Around this time, I had an experience of loosing something very close to me. It was Muffy, our first cat and first pet! As strange as this may seem, loosing Muffy gave me a real life taste, of what it felt like to never see something you loved ever again. Though one of my classmates, who I had sat next to, had died, it wasn't the same when we lost Muffy. I felt a void in my heart that I had never felt before. The whole family loved Muffy; he was a stray cat who became attached to our household. One morning whilst my sisters and I were getting ready for school, Muffy strolled home as usual. Suddenly he started to reach. He was choking. As we tried to help him, he just ran around in circles. We all began to scream.

"Help, help." We all cried hoping someone would hear us. Mum had not yet arrived home from her night shift at the hospital and dad had gone off early to work. So, my big sister ran across the road to the neighbours to get help. My neighbour quickly got his car out of his drive to take us to the vet. But it was too late, Muffy had died. He had choked to death whilst we watched in horror. When mum arrived home, the news upset her so much that she had to take the week of work.

When I was fifteen years old, I had my first boyfriend; Darren. He was not much to look at. He was tall, black, with thick lensed glasses and a pointed chin. But I didn't care, he was my first love. I thought our relationship would never end. I could imagine our wedding day with me walking up the aisle wearing a beautiful dress. Darren would turn to greet me with a warm tender smile. I could see us having lots of children and we could live happily ever after.

Like a fairy tale. But this was not to be. We only lasted six months.

I had acquired a job through Darren's Auntie as a chambermaid at a local bed and breakfast. Darren's Auntie knew the owner, a white lady from a place in Liverpool, who she had been friends with for years, so I didn't have to go through the interview process. It was great to have my independence. To buy the clothes that I wanted. I didn't want to lose my job so I worked hard.

The owner threw a party and we were invited. This is where I got drunk for the first time. Darren's Auntie had made an alcohol concoction.

"Just drink it," she insisted thrusting a large glass in my hand.

I took it and drank the vodka cocktail in one go. It wasn't long before my vision started to blur and my head began to spin. Poor Darren had to watch me kiss and grope his best mate as I couldn't control my actions. I was conscious of what I was doing but couldn't stop. By the end of the night I felt so sick that I threw up all over Darren. He was so angry, he finished with me. I was devastated. I couldn't stop crying for days. I learnt not to drink alcohol to excess again. It takes control of you!

I'd been working at the bed and breakfast for a few weeks when I met the boss's daughter. She was of mixed race, as her dad was black.

"Hello," she said. "My name's Julle, what's yours?"

"Fiona," I replied.

I could tell she was spoilt by the way she spoke to me. She made it clear to me that she was in control. I knew there was going to be trouble.

The bed and breakfast was a large house with many rooms. Julie was meant to help me, but she never pulled her weight. She just bossed me about. One day, whilst I was hoovering the rooms upstairs, Julie called me.

"Fiona."

"Yes?" I answered

"When you've finished could you clean the toilets out?" she asked in a demanding way. I sensed she was telling me rather than asking. But I was busy.

"I'm hoovering upstairs." I replied.
I thought that was the end of our conversation as she never said another word. But her mother came up the stairs.

"Fiona." She said with authority. "Julie has just informed me that you're refusing to clean the toilets out." "Do as you're told," she shouted.
'How dare she,' I thought. 'She's not my mother.'

"Stick your job," I shouted back at her. "Your daughter's nothing but a whore," I told her and demanded the money she owed me.

She was in so much shock she just paid me and I never went back. This attitude ingrained in the depths of my personality for years and I learnt to speak up in this way.

I left school when I was sixteen and went to college, as this seemed the right thing to do. I had played up at school and wanted to do re-takes. I went to study English, Math's and Biology but it only lasted three months. I was subjected to a range of racist insults and abuse.

The last straw was when I was tapping my pencil on my desk and the lecturer said,

"Stop playing with your bongo drums!"
Unsure I heard him right, I continued tapping my pencil.

"Stop playing with your bongo drums!" he repeated.
Shocked and humiliated, I wanted him to feel the same.

"You white bastard," I muttered under my breath.

"What did you say?" he questioned. "Stand up and repeat what you said so the whole class can hear," he insisted.

"You white bastard," I shouted at him, and stormed out. That was the end of college for me.

My conflicting personality, cultural differences, abuse and upbringing were to be the formation of my life.

CHAPTER 2

THE UNEXPECTED TRAP

It was now two months before my seventeenth birthday, and I had no idea of what I wanted to do with my life. College going wrong made me loose all sense of direction, so I spent a lot of my time mixing with people from the black community. Those who also had no focus. I enjoyed reggae music and would go out partying all night, drinking and smoking.

Mum tried to warn me not to go to certain places and mix with certain people, but I wouldn't listen.

"You don't know what they're like," she would often say.
But I didn't care. As a sixteen year old, I thought I knew it all.

I had one particular friend, Beverly, who introduced me to a different world. The world of Rasta's. Beverly was very serious about it. She loved the sensuality of the dark smoky atmosphere. But for me, Rastafarianism was a cultural thing. A way of living and it felt great. There was a hidden understanding that we were one of a kind. A black thing. This made me feel safe. Men and women wore dreadlocks in their hair. Women kept theirs covered by wearing wraps and some dressed in African gowns. I did not adopt this ideal of appearance, but enjoyed their company and went along with the flow of things.

I had known Beverly through out my life. Mum and dad had known her parents when they were in Jamaica. Beverly was a strong willed person, always determined to get her own way. She had a very forceful personality and was overpowering. Although I got on with her, I always felt a bit intimidated by her. Whenever she spoke to me, it was with such authority, that I didn't dare to disagree with her, even if I wanted to. It was her way or not at all.

Beverly was eighteen years old. She had a two year old daughter from a previous relationship and was pregnant with her second child. She had been living in London with her boyfriend, Shaun. They had been together for two years, but now she wanted to leave him and return to Cambridge saying he was not her type of man. He disliked the Rasta way of life. He hated the fact that she wore a wrap around her head and mixed with the Rasta's all the time. This had become the main source of tension between them.

Beverly begged mum to let me go to London with her to pack her clothes. At sixteen, I'd never been to London or in fact, anywhere out of Cambridge without my parents. I remember being excited at the idea of going. Mum trusted Beverly so agreed I could go.

London was so different from Cambridge. It had lots of tall buildings, mainly blocks of flats. There were also a lot more black people. In some areas, there appeared to be more black people than white. Regardless they all seemed to mingle together silently doing their shopping, and commuting together on public transport. Everyone going about their own business with no intimate contact.

Beverly had a room in a shared house in Stretham. Whilst we were there, Beverly decided she didn't want to leave Shaun; she wanted to give their relationship a bit more time, so I phoned mum to let her know I wouldn't be coming home until the next day. This put Mum in a predicament. She did not want me to stay, but she knew I was dependent on Beverly for a lift back. So she agreed it was okay.

That night they took me to a party where we stayed until the early hours of the morning. I had not done this before and had a good time. I didn't dare tell mum I had gone out. As far as she was concerned, Beverly and Shaun had looked after me well. So next time Beverly asked if I could go to London, she said yes. Unfortunately, I didn't know that Beverly had plans for me.

This time we went to Brixton. Beverly took me to the 'front line' to show me where the Brixton riots had taken place. There were still some places boarded up. A reminder of what had happened. She then took me to the home of a male friend of hers. He lived in an old fashion block of flats. Everything was situated upstairs. On entering the front door we had to go straight up a set of stairs which brought us to a landing where the sitting room and kitchen were. On the next floor up, was the toilet/bathroom, then bedrooms on the floor above. The flat was well kept and finely decorated. Her friend seemed to be a man of order. Because he lived on his own, he had his bed in the sitting room. Living and sleeping in there. When we arrived, there were many people in his company.

"Hello Hubert, this is my good friend Fiona from Cambridge." Beverly said as she introduced me.

"Hi," I said sheepishly.

Feeling timid, I could feel my shyness overwhelm me. There were too many strange people in the room for me to cope with.

"Welcome," Hubert greeted as he motioned for me to sit on the bed. There was a strange look in his eyes and he smiled at me in a way that gave me an uneasy feeling.

Hubert was a Rasta man who looked like a well-known black reggae singer. He was tall, dark and slim: about thirty years old and sported a small beard and moustache. He wore a blue tracksuit bottom with white stripes down the sides and a white T-shirt. He had on a tall trilby hat covering a large amount of dreadlocked hair. His appearance was precise.

We weren't there long, when Hubert got up and went out the room. He returned with a large Doberman dog. I shuddered with fear and turned away, scared I was going to be attacked. Hubert paraded the dog proudly in front of me. I was petrified. My mind flooded with images from when I was a child when a neighbour's dog had bitten my hand. Mum had tried to warn me on several occasions.

"Don't go near the fence," her words echoed. But I did not listen.

Beverly laughed at me whilst everyone else in the room sat silently. She could tell by my expressions I was afraid. Hubert led the dog back into the kitchen and shut the door tightly behind him.

Hubert's visitors soon left. Beverly and Shaun chatted away to him while I sat quietly on the corner of his bed. After about half an hour, Beverly went into the hallway and beckoned Shaun.

"We're going to the shops," she shouted to me. "We won't be long."

I did not want to be left alone in Hubert's company but was too afraid to answer back. So I just sat and done as I was told. Like a soldier obeying his commanding officer.

Whilst Hubert went to show them out, beads of sweat formed on my forehead, and I could feel my heart pumping hard. I wasn't confident to call Beverly back and tell her quietly I did not want to be left alone with a man I did not know.

It seemed like a lifetime before I could hear Hubert coming up the stairs. 'Why was he taking so long? And what were they doing?' Lost in my thoughts, the door opened.

"Here are your things." Hubert handed me my over night bag.

"Where's Beverly and Shaun?" I asked.

I could feel the anger boil up inside of me. 'What was Beverly's game? Surely she would never leave me.'

"Them soon come," he replied in his strong Jamaican accent. But they never did.

I sat quietly. Not speaking a word and as the time slowly ticked by, I hoped for every second that Beverly might just turn up.

"Let me take your shoes off for you." He said, breaking the silence, as he bent down to undo the buckle on my sandal.

"No." I said, as I kicked my feet to release them from his grip.

"Beverly will be back soon," I tried to believe.
Hubert kissed his teeth and pulled away angrily. I froze in horror as he stood up and started to strip. Turning away so I did not have to see his naked body, terror gripped me as he moved suddenly towards the bed. 'This cannot be real.' Thank God he pushed past me and jumped under the covers leaving me alone.

I sat still, waiting for him to go to sleep. Tick tock, tick, tock, tick, tock, the clock tormented me, reminding me of the long night ahead of me. I soon became tired, so when I heard Hubert snoring, I went to sleep.

Hearing a shuffle, I opened my eyes. Hubert was awake and it was daylight outside. I believed I was safe as the night was now over.

"Good morning," he greeted me. He had a smile on his face which made me cringe.
Feeling scared, I was not safe after all. My heart pounding fast, Hubert pushed his hand up my skirt. I tried to push

him away but he forced himself on top of me. Hubert had his wicked way. After he finished, he grinned and went to the shop leaving me on my own.

Degraded and humiliated, I couldn't believe my so called friend had set me up like this. To be raped! I wanted to go, but the fear of his Doberman dog jumping up and down on the balcony looking at me, prevented me from leaving. I had no choice, but to sit and wait.

Beverly returned all happy and care free about leaving me.

"Hello, we're back. Did you have a nice time?" she smirked.

"Why did you leave me?" I asked.

"Oh, come on," she said laughing brushing my words aside. "It's time to go home."
Beverly had no consideration for my feelings. I did not say what had happened, I was feeling dirty and ashamed. I questioned myself. 'Was it my fault? Did I do something to make him do this to me? Was it something I had said?' The questions could go on and on with no answers, so I decided the best way to deal with it, was to shut out the pain, and that is what I did.

Back in Cambridge I told mum that I had a good time. I didn't dare tell her what had happened. If she knew she would never let me out again.

CHAPTER 3

THE PAIN GOES DEEPER

I decided to move on from what had happened to me and avoided Beverly's company. My birthday was coming up and I was looking forward to it. Me and my twin had started going to a pub called the Portland Tavern next door to the Pentecostal church we used to go to when we were younger.

The Portland Tavern was a local pub used mainly by the black community. People would come from the surrounding towns, such as, Hitchin, Bedford and Luton for a night out. The pub specialised in catering for the needs of the black community. Playing reggae music, and having dominoes for the older generation. Most people I knew in my culture played dominoes for social enjoyment.

I still had no direction in life but knew I had to work, to look after myself. I could not expect my parents to provide for me the things I desired, things they would see as not needed. Like make up and the latest fashion. So I got myself a weekend cleaning job in a private hospital to tide me over financially.

It was one of those bright Saturday afternoons just before my birthday. The shinning sun brought joy into my heart as I rushed out after work to buy a new dress. I was going to a late night party after the pub had shut. The dress I brought was beautiful. It was white and strapless with an embroidered pattern ingrained in it. I felt pleased with myself, as I had earned it. I hurried home to show off the dress to my sisters and there he was. The best looking man I had ever seen sitting on the sofa in the living room. Oliver was gorgeous!

My dad's friend Andy had brought him round. I had seen Oliver before at the pub and I had always liked him, but had never spoken to him.

Oliver was in the army. He was stationed in Germany. It was his home leave so he'd come to stay at Andy's house in Cambridge. As we looked at each other, there was an instant attraction. I knew he liked me and I liked him. When he smiled at me, there was a twinkle in his eyes and I knew I had to see him again.

"Are you going out tonight?" I asked bravely.

"Yep," he responded.

That was all I needed to know.

Oliver was twenty four years old. Seven years older than me. He had a pleasant character, a beautiful skin tone, red lips, crystal white teeth, was six foot, two inches and stunningly good looking with a few freckles. He had this habit of raising one eyebrow, which made me laugh. I would try to copy him to his amusement. Oliver was a decent guy.

That night, I entered the pub in my white strapless dress and high heeled shoes. I could smell the familiar aroma of marijuana lingering through the air.

"Uhm," I thought as I breathed it in. It smelt good. It was like perfume to me. The music was loud. The DJ was playing our popular song.

'Buffalo soldier, dreadlocks Rasta, strolling from Africa, sold to America, fighting for survival.'

Everyone appeared relaxed. Smoking their joints, rocking side to side with their cans of Special Brew. A surge of excitement rushed through me in the familiar surroundings. I was at home.

After about an hour, I turned my head as if by instinct towards the door just as Oliver walked in. He was perfectly dressed. He wore a grey beret slanted to one side of his face. He looked really good. As soon as he noticed me staring at him, he walked across to where I was standing.

"Wha gawn," he greeted me in the usual Jamaican language. He raised his eyebrow and gave me a cheeky smile which made me laugh.

"I'm fine," I replied shyly.
I was feeling hot inside. My hands were clammy and I could feel beads of sweat form on my forehead. I was feeling nervous, but Oliver put me at ease, and after we had chatted for a while, he asked me to dance.

As we danced, I felt my body stiffen up. Oliver smiled at me. He knew I was shy, so not to embarrass me, suggested we sat down. He proved to be a real gentleman.

Oliver and I spent nearly every moment together, and on my seventeenth birthday we became an item. He was due to finish his leave from the army at the end of March, but we liked each other a great deal and wanted to spend more time together. So Oliver went A.W.O.L. (Absent Without Official Leave).

"Can Oliver stay here please?" I asked mum. "He could sleep on the settee," I further suggested.

Mum liked Oliver. She thought we made a nice couple and would settle down together. So she agreed he could stay.

Oliver and I were getting on great, but unfortunately lurking in the background of our relationship was a woman named Sandra. Sandra was married to Andy so she knew Oliver quite well. She was the same age as Oliver so they had some things in common. Sandra and Andy were going through marital problems. Andy slept around and would be violent towards her. Because of this, we felt sorry for her.

Sandra was a very pretty woman. She had naturally toned lips. When she smiled her face beamed. She had a perfectly poised face with beautiful bright eyes. She presented herself professionally and she wore expensive clothes. Sandra was very attractive.

She had started to befriend me as soon as my relationship started with Oliver. I had vaguely known her before through Andy, but she had never been a friend. Now she was visiting me almost every day, which meant walking from one end of town where she lived, several miles to my parent's house.

At first she was friendly towards me, but then over a short period of time things changed. Sandra would hardly speak to me. She became close to Oliver. She would often sit and whisper in his ear in front of me. I tried to ignore it, refusing to take in what she was doing. I knew her behaviour was not right but was scared of a confrontation in case I was wrong. Besides, no one in my family had mentioned that they had noticed anything. 'Maybe I was imagining it.' I tried to shut out the pain, but my mind kept recalling a time in the past, just before Oliver and I became an item. I had previously made a remark in front of Sandra when she visited my parents with Andy.

"I like Oliver and I'm going to have him," I said jokingly.

"Oh yeah!" Sandra snapped back.

Though her remark had stabbed at my heart, I did not see what she meant by it, and now it seemed clear. Everywhere I went, Sandra was there. If I went out she followed me to the bar, to the toilets and where ever I went. Soon everyone began to notice this. She would copy my clothes and my hair styles. Sandra could afford a lot more than I could. So every time I bought something, she would buy something of better quality, but the same style and colour. It did not actually bother me too much. Although it was a bit unusual. I took this behaviour as a compliment. Besides, I had more important things on my mind. I tried to work out what her motive was. Did she want to gain Oliver's approval because he was Andy's friend? Or was it something more uncanny?

Sandra normally hung around with a group of white girls; Dee, Marie, Paula and Susie who were regulars in the Portland Tavern. They all went out with Oliver's army friends, a group of black guys. Oliver was friendly with them all. It appeared that everyone in his circle of friends were tightly sealed together with me on the outside. Dee would speak to me whenever she saw me but was good friends with Sandra, and would do whatever Sandra advised.

"Sandra said I shouldn't marry Colin," Dee had confided in me.

"Why?" I asked.

"Because she said it would not work because her marriage didn't."

Dee was certain about Sandra's advice. In fact, all her friends would take on her advice without making conscious decisions for themselves. They all looked up to her.

Sandra seemed determined to interfere in our relationship. When I was on my own with Oliver, I felt like we were a couple. But whenever Sandra was around, I would withdraw from him instantly as though she was his partner and I was his mistress, hovering around in the background. It was ridiculous; she would comb his hair, want to cook for him and iron his clothes. It became a strange set up. Eventually, Andy accused them out right of having an affair, which they both denied.

Sandra soon threw Andy out. He had become more violent towards her and she'd had enough. Even though Andy was no longer living with Sandra, Oliver would still leave me at my parent's house; where he was now living and go visit Sandra. There was no real evidence of them having an affair, but I still had my suspicions.

I was naïve and confused. I was blinded to the truth. I refused to see what was happening in front of me.

We had been together about two months when Oliver came to the decision, to hand himself over to the Army. Part of me was devastated. I was besotted with Oliver and didn't want him to go. But the way he had been with Sandra had disheartened and hurt me.

Mum and I drove Oliver to the main barracks in Colchester, where the military police arrested him and put him in the army prison. He was sentenced to four weeks imprisonment and was later shipped back to Germany where he was stationed to finish off his sentence.

I decided to look for a full time job to past the time away. I had gained typing skills whilst at school and wanted to put them into practice. I applied for a job at the Cambridge Science Park as receptionist/typist for a firm that was based there. Whilst waiting to hear back from them, I had some unexpected news.

Oliver had been gone two weeks, when mum asked if I'd had a period.

"I don't know." I replied.

I didn't really understand periods. I didn't know much about them. I didn't know they were meant to happen every month, (especially since I hardly had them), or that you could become pregnant by sleeping with someone unprotected. I hadn't really had the whole 'facts of life' thing explained to me.

"You need to have a pregnancy test, you look pregnant to me," Mum exclaimed.

I thought it was all a joke. But reality kicked in when I phoned up for my test results and was told it was positive. Ironically the job I applied for, phoned me on the same day to tell me I got the job!

I was roughly six weeks pregnant. Dad was devastated at first, but both parents were great and said they would support me. I informed Oliver in Germany as soon as I could. Although he sounded shocked, he said he would stand by me and support me as best he could.

A couple of weeks later, my sister Janet announced she was pregnant too! Dad was overwhelmed. He could not believe two of his young girls were to become mothers. Mum decided that she was going to turn the front room into a downstairs bedroom for me and my twin, so we could have more room when the baby arrived. Mum had it all figured out. Janet would then share her room with Mirianne, whilst Andrea moved into my old room. Our parents stood by both of us. They were great.

I took the job at the Science Park. I was going to need all the money I could get. I didn't tell my new employers I was pregnant in case they withdrew the job offer. I concealed my pregnancy the best I could and left when I could no longer hide it.

I was three months pregnant when I bumped into Beverly. I hadn't seen her for a while and didn't particularly want to now.

"I hear you're seeing Oliver," she spoke enquiringly.
The black community in Cambridge was so small, gossip always got around quickly. Everyone knew each other's business.

"Yes," I replied. Beverly looked like she had something on her mind.

"What's wrong?" I questioned. I could tell she wanted to tell me something.

"Oh nothing," Beverly replied. "Just come round and see me." She looked me up and down before walking off.
I didn't respond. I knew Beverly was up to no good. I didn't want to see her again, but she got me thinking. Curiosity got the better of me, so I decided to pay her a visit the next day.

"Hi Fiona." Beverly welcomed me with a smile as she opened the door. "How are you?"

"Fine thanks," I replied. I wasn't interested in the pleasantries I just wanted to know what she had to tell me. Beverly invited me in and we soon got chatting.

"So how long have you been seeing Oliver?" she asked.

"Oh, a little while. Why?" I replied with a question. I didn't trust Beverly. I could sense there was a hidden motive behind her question.

"Oh nothing," she responded. But I knew there was more.

"What about Sandra," she further enquired.

"What about her?" I snapped. Beverly smiled. She knew she had said something that had caught my attention.

"Oh, nothing," she responded again. Much to my annoyance.

"What were you going to say?" I demanded. "Do you think she's seeing Oliver?"
I'd fell into Beverly's trap. She could see I was suspicious about Oliver and Sandra.

"I don't know they seem a bit close don't they?" she stated, fuelling my insecurity.

"Well, what do you think?" I questioned again.
Beverly never responded. Just left me guessing, with her game playing. When I left, I was close to tears. I could not understand why she was so spiteful towards me. 'How could she be so cruel?' 'Why did she want to hurt me so much?' 'What had I ever done to her?' I was too scared to speak out. To ask why? So I kept my feelings quietly to myself. Twice now I'd had my friendship abused. One had set me up to be raped, and the other was stealing my bloke.

I became guarded, to who I let get close to me. I didn't want it happening again. But it did. This time I was deceived by one of my closest cousins.

Our cousin Jade used to visit us quite a bit. She was a lot older than me and my sisters, so we looked up to her. And because she was my cousin, I trusted her. What a mistake that was.

"She's a creep," Jade sneered one morning whilst at my mum's house.

"Who?" we all asked. My mum and sisters were all in the same room when she said this.

"Sandra, she follows you everywhere you go and copies what you wear." Jade was one of the people who noticed.

"What... does she?" I hadn't really been worried about that, I was more worried about her and Oliver.

"There's something not right about her and Oliver," I told her. It had been weighing heavy on my heart and it had become a burden that I had to bare.

As a family, we discussed the situation. They said they had all noticed, but did not want to say anything to hurt me. We all decided not to say anything, but wait and see what would happen.

The next morning about nine o'clock I got up. I was feeling much better. It was a relief to know others saw the situation the same as I did and it was not my imagination. As I wondered down the stairs the phone rang. It was Sandra. She was at Jade's house. She demanded to come round and speak to the family. She sounded upset.

It wasn't long before there was a bang at the door. Sandra had arrived. She pushed her way into the living room and insisted that we all sat down to hear what she had to say. Jade had told her everything we had spoken about. Sandra insisted her and Oliver's relationship was platonic and she spoke with such firmness and authority that we all just sat in silence as she went on and on, explaining herself without any shame or guilt whatsoever.

"Wait till he gets back, I'm telling him about you lot!" she spitefully said as she got up and walked out, without saying another word.

I was besides myself, I couldn't believe she would make up lies about me and my family without a care for my unborn child. We never confronted Jade. Mum taught us something, 'you have to play a fool to catch wise.' This meant you should behave as though you do not understand to gain more information.

I was four months pregnant when Oliver was granted his home leave. Mum allowed him to stay at our house again.

"I hate the army," Oliver confessed.
He'd become severely depressed. I had never known depression before and didn't know what to do or say. I sat and listened whilst he told me about the hardships he had experienced, and I felt sorry for him.

Before long, before Oliver was spending time at Sandra's house again. I hadn't seen her since the confrontation with me and my family. I knew in my heart she had told Oliver what had happened at my parent's house because we soon drifted apart. We hardly spoke to each other unless it was necessary to do so, and I felt sad and defeated.

A few days before Oliver was due to go back to Germany, mum was doing his washing. She emptied out the pockets to his tracksuit bottoms and found a letter. It was to Sandra. As I read it, a bit stuck in my mind. The truth was there, staring me in the face. 'What is it you want from me?' He wrote. 'Is there any chance of us getting together properly?'

My fears were confirmed. My heart felt like it had been ripped out. Mum told me to keep quiet about the letter. "Focus on your future," she advised.

Because of mum's strength, I had the confidence to keep this secret to myself. I decided not to tell anyone that I had seen the letter. I knew deep down, Oliver and Sandra would deny it, if I confronted them. Even with the evidence.

Oliver soon went back to Germany. He was due to leave the army completely, in the New Year. Whilst he was away, I prepared for the arrival of my baby.

Rueben was born in the month of January, and weighed a healthy 9lbs 2oz. Mum was with me when I gave birth. It was not easy becoming a mother especially for the first time without the father around. Thank God, I had the help and support of my parents and my sisters.

When Rueben was one month old, Oliver left the army for good and returned to England but he didn't help me with Rueben as promised. If mum had not been there for me and bought the things Rueben needed, he would not have had anything.

Oliver soon became paranoid. He accused my parents of listening to our conversations and of talking about him behind his back. His behaviour was totally out of character. I assumed his paranoia had something to do with what Sandra had told him. But I was to find out I was wrong.

Rueben was only two months old, when I was cleaning out our bedroom. I took Oliver's suitcase from the top of the wardrobe. I couldn't help myself, and I looked anxiously through it. I found several letters addressed to Oliver. Curiosity got the better of me, so I read them.

Some were from Sandra whilst Oliver was in Germany. They included photos of her but by this time I did not care. I just wanted the whole situation to end. I just wanted to get on with my life, with my baby, who I loved more than anything in the world.

I continued to open some more letters. To my amazement I discovered some love letters written to Oliver from a German girl. There was also a ferry ticket to Germany dated for some time in April, for Oliver to go and be with this girl. I could not believe it. No wonder he was paranoid. Oliver had plans for his life and it did not include me or Rueben. I did not inform him of my discovery. I kept quiet and carried on as normal.

While waiting for the day in April to arrive, Oliver became more and more paranoid. He continued to accuse my mum and dad of talking about him behind his back. I didn't know how he dare, knowing what he had planned.

A week before he was due to leave, Oliver said cunningly,

"I'm going to move to London. I feel homesick," he lied.

Oliver was born and brought up in London. It was his hometown so it was easy for him to use this as an excuse to leave me. But I knew it was part of his plan to escape.

"Alright then," I agreed. "I know you've been unhappy here for a long time now. You will visit won't you?" I asked in anticipation of his answer.

"Yes. Of course," Oliver replied smugly.

Rueben was now three months old. Oliver did come to visit once that week, but he didn't really pay much attention to Rueben. Not that I cared. I just wanted him to hurry up and go, so I could get on with my life.

"When are you coming back?" I asked slyly, as he got up to go.

"I'll write," Oliver replied.

"You'll write!" I snapped back.

"Uh, no, I mean I'll call you," he stuttered, pointing to the phone in my parent's hallway, trying to cover his tracks.

"Okay," I said casually. I'd had enough. We kissed goodbye as usual and he left. I knew it was the last time I was going to see him.

Two weeks had gone by when I received a letter. It was stamped from Germany and had a German address on the back. I knew it was from Oliver. Oliver explained what I had supposedly said behind his back. He accused me for the breakdown of our relationship. I was so angry I wrote back.

'Dear Oliver,

I hope when you receive this letter that you are in good health. It was a pity you didn't tell me you were going. I already knew you were due to catch the ferry at 4pm to Germany on the ... of April, but I was hoping you would not decide to take the coward's way out and have the decency to tell me what your intentions were.'

I went on to explain that I also knew who had been telling him lies about me and my family. He further betrayed me and forwarded them my letter.

Not long after this incident, I went to the pub. It was my first time out since giving birth. Sandra, Dee, Paula and the other girls were there. I looked towards them and smiled at them but they all ignored me. I knew it was because of Sandra. She had won this battle. I was left feeling like I'd been sentenced for something I did not do.

A few months had passed. I'd been invited to a party and decided to go. I had not been out in ages because of what happened at the pub. At the party, standing in the corner I spotted him. Hubert. Fear gripped me as the past came flooding back. As soon as he saw me, he headed in my direction.

But then..."You have to come home. Rueben needs you." I heard my dad's voice as he approached me from behind. What a relief.

In the early hours of that morning there was a knock on my bedroom window. As I peered through the curtains, looking out the window, my eyes met his. It was Hubert. Cautiously I asked him what he wanted. He said he'd come to stop the rumours. Beverly had told him I was pregnant and because of what happened he thought the baby could be his. Foolishly, I let him in. I just wanted to shut her up. He took one look at Rueben and knew he was not his. I never saw him again after that.

I discovered later that Jade had also slept with Oliver when I was pregnant. She had diverted the attention off herself towards Sandra as a cover up. I learnt the hard way. 'Just because someone says they're your friend, it does not mean they are.' A harsh lesson to learn!

I left home at the age of eighteen, damaged by the control of others. Rueben was now ten months old; it was time for me to be independent. I tried to get on with my life by picking up the pieces and move on. Deep down in my heart I knew I had not done anything wrong. I was the victim, of a web of deceit and it did not feel nice. Throughout all my ordeals I didn't cry. All my emotions were bottled up. Until one day I felt desperate, unloved and rejected by a world that appeared full of hate. The pain in my heart had now gone deeper and I had nowhere to put it. I sobbed uncontrollably. Afterwards, once again, I carried on, as though nothing had happened and got on with my life, keeping all that I felt to myself.

CHAPTER 4

WHEN THE SEED WAS SOWN

My first home was a two-bedroomed maisonette. It had a medium sized sitting room and a small kitchen. It was sufficient for Rueben and me. Unfortunately there was no central heating and the building was old. Many of the walls were covered with mildew, but it was home. With the help of mum and dad, I decorated it the best way I could. Because I didn't have a job, I was entitled to government payments to help bring up Rueben. This was not much, but it helped. Unconfident about my new responsibilities, I relied on my parents financially and would mostly stay at their house. My place seemed empty and I would be afraid. I was used to living with lots of people so I only slept at my house if someone stayed with me.

After a few months, I soon began to feel more confident about staying at my new home. Rueben was now a bit older. Walking and saying a few words. Life was a bit easier and I didn't feel so tied down. The past was left behind and I was starting to feel alive again until one day there was a knock at the door. 'Why don't you just go away?' I thought. It was Beverly. My past had come to haunt me.

"Hi, I thought I'd come and see you," she claimed as I opened the front door.

I stood for a moment staring at Beverly. I wanted to know her motive. She appeared uncomfortable. Feeling nothing but pity for her, I reluctantly invited her in. I could not be nasty to her. No matter what had happened, it was not in my nature. Beverly stepped in and appeared shocked.

"Gosh! Isn't you home lovely," she gasped.

Beverly had a thing about people's homes. So I assumed she just came round to be nosey.

"Well done. You've done a good job Fiona," she commented.

"Thanks," I replied, feeling confident about my home.

She seemed to have changed, so in my heart, I decided to give her a second chance. Life was really going well for me. There would be no room for her to do any damage. So I thought!

Soon Beverly starting visiting me on a regular basis. Sometimes she would bring her sister Serena with her. My sister Janet would visit often too. Janet had given birth the same time as me. All four of us were single mums on government benefits and we all had small children. Every so often we would take it in turns to go round each other's house for dinner, but mostly we would meet at my house. We would spend the night drinking, smoking and listening to reggae music. At the weekend we would rush around to find babysitters for the children so we could go out. I would tell mum I was going out and pretend I had a babysitter. Mum didn't want anyone else to babysit so she would always volunteer.

We were all into the Rasta vibes and would travel all over the place going to parties in London, Hitchin, Slough, Peterborough. Anywhere there was a reggae dance happening. My sisters Natasha and Andrea would also come. Life was never boring. Some of the clubs we went to consisted of people who had lost all sense of reality. If you trod on someone's shoes you could get shot. Once, when we were at a dance, there were gunshots. Everyone ran to one side of the club. No one left. Everyone continued enjoying their evening when the excitement had calmed down. This was perfectly normal.

We all got on so well and as a group we used to talk about things in the past. It seemed easier to be honest.

"I have something to tell you," Beverly said looking at Natasha.

"What is it?" Natasha asked.

"When you were with Michael," she confessed, "He slept with Della at my house on the settee."

Michael was a Rasta man from Chelmsford who Natasha had been going out with on a steady basis for months. She had ended up leaving him because he became possessive and abusive towards her. Della was someone we had known most of our lives.

Fortunately for Beverly, Natasha forgave her. The past was left in the past and no more was said. I couldn't believe it. First she'd deceived me, now my sister. It was as if her manipulative personality empowered her to get away with whatever she did.

I began to smoke weed on a regular basis. It didn't cost much for a small bag and I enjoyed getting stoned, as it helped to block out reality and the bad memories. Nearly everyone I knew smoked and enjoyed the Rasta vibes. We all began to wrap our hair with material, like the Rasta women did. We would have different colours and patterns to match our outfits. I was wrapping mine as a fashion thing, following my peers. A male friend of mine bet me five pounds to dread my hair for a month. I won the bet though it was hard not combing my hair for a month.

On the other side of town, Sandra and her little sister had become devoted Rastafarians. They understood what it meant and had decided to dedicate their lives to it. The whole Rasta culture was in full swing amongst us all. Even though I did not fully understand it, for me it was more a black person's thing.

One day there was a loud persistent knocking on the door. I hurried to see who it was. Looking through the key hole in anticipation, I saw Beverly looking flustered.

"Quick, guess what?" she said as I opened the door.

"What's happened?" I questioned.

"It's Sandra; she wants us all to meet up at my house. She wants to see us. It's serious."

'Here we go again,' I thought. I could feel the past creeping up from the back of my mind.

"No. If she wants to see me she can come here." I was determined that Sandra was not going to get her own way with me. Not this time.

Beverly, Serena and all my sisters met up at my house. Waiting for Sandra to arrive, I prepared myself for battle.

"You've been talking about me," she said when she arrived. "And your mum's been slagging me and my children off," she bellowed, as if she was in charge of everyone.

Someone was stirring up trouble again. All that she said was untrue. I didn't care what she was saying. This person had walked all over me where my son's dad was concerned and now she was sitting in my home accusing me and my family of something we had not done. I sat there in silence, indifferent to what she was saying, then I finally responded to her accusations.

"I haven't done anything wrong," I told her.

Sandra went quiet for a moment as though she'd caught my words.

"What have I said about you?" I questioned.

Sandra didn't answer. She continued to go on and on about the people who were close to her, and who had slept with her husband behind her back. She had obvious issues which she was taking out on us, unjustly.

After Sandra had left, I had my suspicions, it was Beverly's doing. She was very manipulative. But I still mixed with her as she continued to subtly intimidate me.

Towards the end of summer, I had arranged to go to a big dance held at Milton Keynes. No one in our group could drive so we arranged for a male friend of ours to take us. It was a big event and we were determined not to miss out. This is where I met my first Rasta boyfriend, Simeon.

Simeon was a very serious man. He was older than me which I liked. Though he took great care of me, I didn't take our relationship seriously. On our first date I took Beverly with me.

"He's nice," Beverly commented. "You're lucky."
It seemed a good thing to be going out with a Rasta man. Though I couldn't see why. It made no difference to me as long as they were black. White men did not come into my mind. I did not cross the threshold of my own race.

Every time Simeon came to visit, I would laugh. I found his seriousness fascinating. He lived a Rasta life. Devotional. He was a vegetarian, smoked lots of weed, showed love and had dread locks. This was my interpretation of what a Rastafarian did.

Me and Beverly enjoyed the buzz of being around Simeon and his friends, who were major hustlers, selling large quantities of weed. This was normal for them and I could not see anything wrong with what they were doing especially as I smoked it. One time Natasha came with me to Simeon's flat, which he shared in the middle of Harlston, London, with a group of Rasta's. The flat had bars up against the door and was heavily bolted. No one could enter unless they were close friends otherwise they would be well interrogated and since they had knives and guns no one dared to cross them. Despite this, they felt nervous by the presence of me and my twin, especially when we both stared at them at the same time because of our similarities.

"Look at the twins. They're frightening," one man commented.

My sister and I were privileged that these men felt like this about us. It meant we were secure.

I continued to go to parties with Simeon. Beverly would always come with me. But soon I had suspicions that Simeon was using me.

"Just strap the weed around your son's waist," he said. "I promise, I'll pay for everything."

Simeon wanted me to go to Jamaica, all expenses paid to smuggle some weed into England for him. If he cared he for me, he would never have suggested I use my son in this way. I could no longer have a relationship with him. So after his proposition, I did not see him again.

"Mum," I cried as I stood in the phone box. "I don't know what to do. I'm pregnant." I always told mum everything. Here I was pregnant by a man I did not intend to see again.

The situation was made all the more desperate by the fact that I had recently had a coil fitted. I had been on the pill in the past but I was not responsible enough, as I kept forgetting to take them. Now I had taken extra measures and still fell pregnant!

"You can't have it," Mum told me.

"I can," I cried.

"Are you mad? What if something is wrong with it?" Mum was clearly worried. I hadn't even considered the possibility, but it made me think, 'what if mum was right?' I had heard stories that a baby could be deformed if a coil was stuck in the wrong place.

I went and got checked out by the doctor. He was concerned as he couldn't find the coil. He said it could be stuck anywhere. It might even be stuck in the baby's head. 'What if it was?' I couldn't take the chance. I was made to feel, an abortion, was the best thing to do. Besides, the law stated it was an acceptable thing to do, so on this thought, I terminated my pregnancy. I felt awful and questioned as to whether I had done the right thing, but it was too late to dwell on it. I had to carry on. Another trauma to be stored!

By the end of the year the issue of God came into my life and the reality of heaven and hell. Me, and Natasha had made friends with another group of Rasta men from Sheffield. None of them were our boyfriends. They were kind, caring and gentle in nature. They were good speakers and we were interested in what they had to say. They went through the book of revelation from the bible with us. It was the first time I was introduced to this book.

"The pope is not a man of God," they claimed.

"And the monarchy is going to fall," they told us.

"Be careful of the beast whose number is six, six, six, marked on his forehead."

"Britain represents Babylon."

If this was true, meant we were living in a country, which was destined for destruction.

This information was frightening. I asked Beverly if what they had said was true. I thought she'd know because of her Rasta connection.

"Yeah, it's true. When God comes, He's coming to judge the world and those who are bad will go to hell. A place of fire," she said.

This frightened me even more.

"Where will I go?" I asked.

"You're a good person. You won't go to hell, you'll go to heaven."

Feeling reassured, it was good to know that Beverly considered me a good person and that I would be going to heaven. A place of peace and tranquility.

Natasha was intrigued by the things the Rasta men told us about the bible. She wanted to know more, so arranged for a bible study to be held at my house. Two Christian women, from the congregation of the church we used to go to when we were younger, came round. Natasha was more enthusiastic than me about learning the word of God, and a competition soon arose between her and Beverly as to who knew more about the bible. I just went along with everything, staying in the background, taking in what I could. The New and Old Testament confused me. I saw them as two different books and this left a question mark in my mind. 'Why was the bible divided?' Although this was the case, the message that had the most impact on me was what our Rasta friends had told us from the book of revelation. 'Those who were not of God would have the mark of the beast stamped on their forehead.'

I eventually lost interest in the Rastafarians, (and stopped wrapping my hair), becoming more intrigued by the Christian community.

One day me, Natasha and a friend of ours, Nadine from school, decided to go to the church convention. A church convention is where many churches gather to celebrate Jesus. It normally takes place once or twice a year. Most of the black community in Cambridge would attend. But mum and dad never went.

The church was packed with people singing and praising God. Banging their tambourines and clapping their hands and shouting 'hallelujah.' When the Pastor preached, it was a profound message.

"If anyone needs prayer feel free to come up to the front," he shouted with passion for Jesus.
Natasha, Nadine and I went up to the altar and knelt down to be prayed over.

"In the name of Jesus give yourselves up. You don't know when He's coming. It could be tomorrow. What are you going to do? Repent and be baptized so you may enter the kingdom of heaven," he shouted again.

The preacher succeeded in putting the fear of God in us; it felt as though God was coming there and then. I did not understand how Jesus had died for us and always thought;

'What if these people worshipped God all their life, missing out on what I thought was fun, to find nothing there?'

Despite this thought, I decided to get baptized along with Natasha and Nadine. We were rushed round to the back of the church where the Pastor spoke to us. Then we were ushered into the basement, changed into white clothes and then submerged into what they called, Holy Water. I did not feel as though I knew what I was doing and the whole thing felt false. Though I had looked at what both sides had to say, the Rasta's and the Christians, I did not understand any of their perceptions about God, but Natasha obviously did. On giving her testimony, Natasha spoke up about her beliefs.

"I've tried Rasta and it's not for me. Jesus is the only way," she claimed.

This did not please Beverly, who was standing at the back of the church, and as we left, Beverly confronted Natasha about what she had said. A big uproar took place about my sister's testimony.

"How dare you say that about Rasta's," Beverly snapped.

"You're nothing but the devil," Natasha shouted back.
It was the first time anyone had stood up against her. Beverly was shaken!

I did not care whether it was the Rasta way or the Jesus way. I had listened to both and none of them made sense to me. No one explained about God and who He is. It just seemed like you had to be a certain way and that was that.

The following week we went to church. I tried to be good during the week by giving up smoking. Trying to do the right thing. At church, I discovered there were rules. As I walked in, we were told that we could not wear jewellery or make up and when Rueben started crying, they got irritated with him and I was sent to the back of the church, where I could hardly hear the sermon. I could not understand or relate to what they were saying so I got up and left.

Disappointed, the following week I didn't go to church, instead I went back to the Portland Tavern.

I soon forgot about God and moved into darkness, falling away from the seed that was sown.

Beverly stopped coming to visit me. Natasha had scared her off. It wasn't long before I was back to my irresponsible self again. I just wanted to have fun. I would go off to London with Natasha and Nadine with a one way ticket and no money. Forgetting I was a mother. We would find a club, rave all night then find someone who was willing to drive us back home to Cambridge. When we reached our destination we'd leave them stranded. It was a game for us. I felt like church had let me down. I was on a self destructive path even though I partied a lot, I was still finding it hard to speak up for my self, and lacked confidence. Whenever we went out I would stand in the corner and not speak to anyone. Soon I became quietly depressed. Sometimes I would lay in bed all day trying to force myself to cry to relief the tension I was feeling, but the tears would not come. I had no future and no vision as to where I was going.

CHAPTER 5

VIOLENCE AND CONTROL

IT was the spring months, when my life changed. It was like a new era for me. My social life had settled down and the people I had been mixing with were now in my past. I started socialising with my cousins whom I had grown up with. They were caring and kind and encouraged me to live decently. We would spend our days taking our children out, shopping and looking after ourselves, and our homes. We would only go out on Friday nights to the Portland Tavern as a break from the children.

Although life was stable by the time summer arrived I was getting bored. I was a single mum with no job and no future, so I began seeking advice from spiritual books, looking for hopeful predictions in my life. These books contained oracles, and different things for divine uses. Divination using playing cards was one such use. As my confidence grew in the reading cards, people started wanting me to do readings for them. Every card I picked had a personal meaning and seemed to be true.

One day while reading the cards, there was the prediction that I was going to meet a man with light skin complexion and there would be love making. I re-did the cards and the reading said the same thing again.

"I can't believe this," I exclaimed to Natasha and Nadine. "Both readings say the same thing."

"Oh yeah!" they exclaimed. Excitement rushed through me - waiting for the evening to come was almost painful.

That evening I went out. I felt good about myself. For the first time in my life, I liked myself. No one was controlling me or telling me what to do, I felt free. I dressed in white and yellow striped shorts that night, with a yellow top and matching yellow head band. Putting on my high heeled sandals, I felt confident that I looked good.

As I entered the Portland Tavern, heads turned. Feeling the people I was mixing with valued me, for once I felt treated as a person and not a toy.

That night I danced with confidence and it did not go unnoticed. A man from a group of men approached me.

"My friend likes you," he stated as he pointed to a tall man with wet curly hair.

Looking across to where they were standing, I knew instantly that I didn't fancy him.

"Come over and say hello," the man encouraged me.

I felt flattered to be picked out from the group I was with, so I went over. The other men looked me up and down admiring me. It felt good to be the centre of attention.

"Hi, my name's George. What's yours?" the man introduced himself politely.

"Fiona," I responded shyly.

"Do you want to go to a party in Hitchin tonight?" he asked.

"I'll have to ask my friends if they want to go," I replied. After a discussion with my friends, we agreed we would go at closing time. We all used to go to Hitchin to parties, so we were familiar with the area. It turned out the men were from there, and they had come to Cambridge for a change of scenery.

At the party George's friend caught my attention. He was clean, but rugged and that was what I liked. He had nice clean teeth which enhanced his smile, and when he laughed his eyes beamed with joy. This attracted me to him.

Terence was so lively, he laughed and joked and appeared to know what he was doing. I ignored George and danced with him all night. We got on like a 'house on fire.' So when the night was over; we arranged to meet up the following night. My card prediction had come true and I began a relationship with him.

Terence was thirty three years old. Thirteen years my senior. He was born in Jamaica and had come to England at the age of thirteen. His grandmother who was bringing him up was finding it difficult to look after him due to his bad behaviour. She thought it would be best if he came to England to live with his father. Terence's father was very strict and used to beat him for every little thing, whilst his step brother was treated differently. This left deep resentment in Terence, and as he grew older, it had a dramatic impact on his personality and his behaviour.

Terence was an old fashioned type of person who believed in the traditional values that a man was the head of the household, doing male duties like decorating, gardening, and other DIY jobs, along with providing for his family legitimately through work. He was a self-employed roofer and a painter and decorator. He saw a woman's role as washing, cooking, ironing, and looking after the children. This is how I thought things were meant to be, so I enjoyed being in a relationship with him, even though we did not live together. The future looked bright.

Terence enjoyed singing to Rasta music. He would say he was a bald head Rasta, meaning he was a Rasta on the inside but not on the outside. I still had no idea what Rasta really meant, so it had no bearing on me. Terence liked to drink and party. I was never bored.

One night whilst being wined and dined, Terence confessed to me that he was a father of four boys. He said he had split up from their mother a few years ago. I accepted this as I had a child from a previous relationship myself, which Terence accepted.

"Have you had a girlfriend since?" I questioned.

"Yes, but I caught her in bed with a friend of mine so I battered him with a baseball bat."

"Really, how could she do that to you? You're so nice," I commented. Not thinking about what he had done to the bloke.

"I nearly killed him," he continued. "And he ended up in hospital."

"Didn't you get into trouble for it?" I asked.

"Yes. I've just come out of prison for attempted murder," he confessed.

Some girls would run a mile at hearing this, but not me. I saw his actions as a 'crime of passion' and empathised with him. He seemed so nice and caring. I couldn't see any violence in him.

We had been together for a few months when I found out I was pregnant. Terence was pleased. We were close and everything felt settled. There was no need for me to worry about him supporting me. We went everywhere together. Mum would look after Rueben at the weekends so I was free to go out with him. The whole family liked Terence. He took care of me; he brought me gifts and paid for everything. He would boost my confidence by the things he said.

"I love you," he would shout out, at parties.

"This is my wife," he would say as he introduced me.

Terence made me feel so special. Life seemed great apart from one thing. Whenever we went out he would flirt and dance closely with my friends sensually, as though they were an item. I would cringe every time he did this, wanting to scream, 'help.' But once again, I kept quiet and watched and accepted it.

I was once warned about Terence at a friend's daughter's Christening party.

"Don't have anything to do with him," she shouted in front of Terence.

"Why?" I asked.

"He beats up women. I'm friends with his children's mother, and he always beats her up."

"I don't believe you. They're not together," I answered, thinking she just wanted to spoil my happiness.

"They live together," she announced.

I refused to believe what she was saying; as far as I was concerned, she was lying. He was very attentive to me, never violent, and would come to Cambridge, and spend the weekends with me, and also the odd night during the week because of his work, where he lived.

I was roughly five months pregnant. Terence and I had spent the day at my parent's house, a habit we'd got into since the beginning of my pregnancy. It had been a good day.

"Let's go out," Terence suggested.

"Okay," I agreed.

It was nice to go down the Portland Tavern in the afternoon. It would be quiet with hardly any people there. So we could relax and play pool... Just the two of us.

On this particular day, my friend Gerald was playing music there. I had not seen him for some time. He was someone my family knew quite well. Whilst Terence went to get our drinks, I went over to say hello.

"Hi, you're getting big now," he said as he greeted me with a big smile.

"Yes I'm five months now. How are you?"

Slap! Terence had taken me by surprise and slapped me around the face.

"What have I done?" I asked, stunned by his action.

Slap! Terence hit me again! I went into shock and could not speak. Gerald looked on in horror but said nothing. I looked around; there were a few people in the pub. It didn't look as though anyone had seen what had happened. I sat down, still, in disbelief whilst Terence stood at the bar, watching my every move. My friend Nadine turned up and I told her what had just occurred. She was disgusted.

"He doesn't scare me," she scowled, glaring at Terence and refused to leave my side for the rest of the evening.

"What do you want to drink?" Terence finally asked me in an aggressive manner. He had not spoken to me until that moment.

"Nothing," I replied. But the look on his face told me if I did not accept the drink, I would be in trouble.

"I'll have a Bacardi and coke," I stuttered still trembling with fear and disbelief over what had just occurred. I was in shock. Terence had changed. I had known him to be laughing, joking, loving and caring, not this aggressive person he'd shown me.

In the back of my mind I could hear the words of the lady at the christening. 'He's always hitting her.' I chose to block them out.

Terence approached me. Without saying a word, he ushered me outside to his car. He spoke by expressions and hand gestures. Silence was my punishment. I wished he would speak. Tell me what I had done wrong. But he was cold towards me. I could feel the ice in the air. He accelerated the car down the motor way. Terence was not taking me home, instead he drove to Hitchin, I was in his territory now.

Terence took me to a party. The warmth from being among so many people gave me a feeling of security. Terence was still not talking to me. In the hustle and bustle of the party, I felt isolated. I did not know any one and I did not have any money to get back home.

"Hello Terence." It was George, happy, full of fun and laughter.

When the opportunity arose, I confided in him.

"You alright?" George had asked.

"No, not really," I responded looking into his face. I could feel the tears well up in my eyes.

"Terence hit me."

"It's got nothing to do with me," George replied, walking away to join the party.

Shocked at his response, I fought back the tears and waited for the night to end.

I watched as Terence spent the night laughing and joking with his friends. I was invisible to him. My back and feet were painful due to the pregnancy, but I had to wait for Terence to be ready. I was too scared to disturb him. At the end of the night, Terence ushered me into the car as before and took me home. He still did not speak to me and I didn't dare say a word.

As he cuddled up to me in bed that night, he whispered in my ear, "I love you," and this made me feel bit better. At least he did care. The incident was never mentioned again and the only other person I told was Natasha. It was our secret.

During the months the next couple of months, I spent most my time at home preparing for my unborn baby, and spending time with Rueben. Rueben was nearly three and a half years old. He'd grown so quickly and I did not realise how lonely he was. Being a young mum meant bringing up a child whilst I was growing up myself, and learning about life. I was not mature and always put my needs first, especially when it came to love. I was looking for Terence's love and Rueben was looking for mine. So when I gave birth to his sister, Keisha, I thought it would be a good idea for him to play with the other children in the neighbourhood at front of our house.

One day whilst Rueben was out playing, I heard a big bang. I ran towards the front door to discover it was shut. The front door was always kept open so I could keep an eye on him. 'Who shut the door?' I thought as I opened it. To my horror, a group of slightly older white boys who lived nearby were beating Rueben up. They decided they did not like him because of the colour of his skin and had called him names. Later, I went to one of the boy's homes, but his mother showed no remorse for what her child had done. As she stared me blankly in the face, I knew then I was fighting a losing battle. I was consoled by a neighbour who had lived their long before me, who was not English herself. She said they were always like that, causing trouble and not to worry.

There were many other situations. Not just for Rueben but also for me.

"I'm looking for Fiona Lynch," I heard someone asking a neighbour for me.

"Oh, you mean the blackies who live there," she remarked...

I was so upset. The neighbour was a little old lady who always spoke nicely to me. A friend, who was visiting me at the time, confronted her. She did not deny what she said and apologised. I could see she did not think she had said anything wrong. She was ignorant about our culture.

Race issues were still a problem, but I was blinded to it. I still only mixed within my own community, so I did not see how much it was there.

As time went on and I spent more and more time at home, the awareness that I lived in a racist community soon became uncomfortable for me and I wanted to move. At night, not far up the road skinheads used to hang around by a block of flats. This meant if I needed anything at the shops, I didn't dare go, for fear of my life.

Terence liked the fact that I spent most my time at home. He had become very possessive and more violent towards me. Unfortunately I did not have anyone close to me, to tell about his violence. Natasha, had moved to London. She knew how aggressive and possessive he was towards me. One time we even discussed how we could get rid of him. It was that bad.

On several occasions, he jumped on my stomach. The pain of his body weight crushing down on me was immense. Other times he would smack my head against the wall, causing me to worry about having brain damage. I was so scared; I had to be careful of what I said. He would be laughing and joking one minute, then screaming and shouting the next. One time he poured a glass of milk over me in front of his brothers for no reason. They were disgusted with his behaviour and could not believe their brother was like that.

It wasn't long before I lost all my friends because of Terence. They were scared of him. If he came to visit and they were at my house, he would be moody, making them feel uncomfortable. If a man I knew spoke to me, he would be very vindictive and cruel to me. He'd make me pay for it. Once at a pub where my dad's friend worked, his son offered me a cigarette. I accepted. Terence looked at me, laughed and walked off out of the pub. 'Oh no,' I thought, realising I was in trouble.

"Terence wants you outside," stated a doorman.
My heart began to pound. I knew something was coming even though I'd done nothing wrong.

Terence was standing in the doorway outside. He looked suspicious. Smash! Everything went black, and I could see stars in front of my eyes. Terence had hit me over the head with a bar stool. As he swung for me again I ducked and ran. I could hear him chasing after me.

"Ouch!" I screamed. "Get off me." I could feel the pain plunging through the top of my head, as he grabbed hold of my hair as tight as he could. He then dragged me down the street towards his car.

"Hey, leave her alone," I heard a shout. Terence let go of my hair. I could see a group of about seven men running towards us.

"Get lost," Terence screamed back, holding a metal pole in his hand which he had pulled out of the boot of his car.
The men began to run as Terence chased them down the road waving the pole menacingly.

Crumpled on the ground where Terence left me, I looked up and saw the ugliness in his face. Pure evil.

"Ugh! Please don't hurt me. Terence, please."
I begged and begged as he pulled me up and pushed me up against the car whilst he unlocked the door. Terence then threw me in the car as though I was luggage. As his eyes caught mine, they pierced right through my soul.

There was silence once again as we travelled to my house. I had to think quickly, The children were at home with a babysitter. I was scared for our lives.

The tyres of the car screeched, as the car came to a halt in the car park near my house. I quickly jumped out of the car and legged it as fast as I could down the pathway to my home. I had to get in before Terence. I could hear the pang of the metal pole as it bounced onto the concrete. Terence had thrown it at me!

Knock, knock, knock.

"Open the door," I pleaded with my babysitter as I looked through the letterbox.
I could see the fear in my babysitters face, peering back at me.

"Open it. Please, Terence's is going to hurt me." Terence was now about twenty steps away from me.
My baby sitter quickly opened the door and shut it, leaving him outside. I ran up the stairs into the bathroom and locked the door behind me. I looked up at the bathroom window. 'That's it', I thought... I'm going to jump through it.

"Open the door, or I'll kick it down," he shouted. My babysitter had let him in.
Petrified, my body did not know what it wanted to do.

"Fiona, come out of the bathroom, I'm scared." My babysitter's frightened voice jolted me back to reality.
It was not fair. She was afraid, and I had to protect her. An inner strength entered me. I was responsible for her well-being, so I opened the bathroom door after Terence had promised, that he would not touch me.

Sitting quietly in the sitting room, Terence glared at me before suddenly jumping up, lunging towards me.

"No Terence, No," screamed my babysitter.

Terence had picked up the chair he was sitting on and had swung it to hit me. She stopped him just in time. He then changed. He switched from being violent and angry, to calm, caring and loving. The side of him that I liked. Everything seemed all right again.

The racial harassment, in the community where I lived, and lack of space in my small maisonette, began to depress me. Moving was the only answer, so I pushed for a move on these grounds. The housing officer was sympathetic, and I was offered a council house, on the other side of Cambridge. This meant a fresh start for me. I could not wait to see it.

I was at my mum's, when Serena arrived and offered to take me to have a look. I never went anywhere apart from mum's and dad's and my sisters, so if Terence turned up to visit me, he would know where to go.

"Wow, look Serena, its beautiful."

My new home was a newly built three bed roomed house with central heating, and freshly painted. Downstairs consisted of a sitting room, dining room, downstairs toilet and a kitchen. Upstairs had a bathroom and three bedrooms. One at the front which would be my bedroom, and two at the back which would be for Rueben and Keisha. This was a palace, compared to my maisonette with no heating, and moss all over the walls.

"You're very lucky, I'm pleased for you," Serena encouraged.

"Let's pop in and say hi, to my mum on the way home," she suggested. Her parents lived around the corner from my new home.

"What time is it?" I enquired. Not wanting to be too long in case Terence visited.

"We haven't been that long; we could go for ten minutes."

"All right," I agreed, nervously, feeling I was doing something wrong.

About five minutes later at Serena's mum's house, the phone rang.

"Fiona, it's for you," called Serena's mum from her dining area. "It's your mum."

"Hi mum." I was cheerful, and was just about to tell her about my new home.

"You'd better come home now. Terence is here, and he's angry because you're not at home."

Mum sounded in a panic. She was usually happy, but this time her voice was trembling and she seemed concerned. I knew I was in trouble. Terence travelled from Hitchin to Cambridge to see me. He would never tell me when he was coming. He just expected me to be at home, and not go anywhere, or socialise with anyone.

"Alright mum, I'll be there right away," I reassured her.

I hurried from Serena's not knowing what I was going to be faced with.

When we arrived at my mum's house, I was relieved to see that Terence's car was not there. I felt safe, thinking he would not be able to get me. We were just about to get out of the car, when suddenly there was a screech of tyres. As I looked, Terence was already out of his car, storming towards me.

"Where have you been? You slut," Terence shouted as I opened the car window.

Thump! Terence punched me on the nose. He didn't care that he was outside my parents' house. He was angry and that was that. I quickly wound up the window so he could not get to me. Serena's son, who was sitting in the back of the car with me and Rueben, began to cry.

"Mum, mum," he sobbed as Serena jumped out of the car, locking the doors with us inside.

She went to knock my mum's front door to alert her to the situation.

"Open the car," Terence shrieked at Serena.

"No," Serena shouted back. "You're frightening my child."

"I don't care. If you don't open the car, I'll smash it up," he screamed at her, as he opened the boot of his car to get something out.

Mum heard the commotion from inside the house.

"What's going on?"

"It's Terence," Serena explained, "Fiona daren't get out the car. He keeps threatening her."

"Terence why you are so wicked?" asked mum. "Get inside; I don't want this sort of commotion in front of my neighbours."

Terence resigned himself to what mum had said, and walked towards the front door. I did the same, but unfortunately, I got too close. Punch! I could feel the wetness of blood all over my face. Terence had punched me in the face right in front of my mum. Blood was pouring from my nose. Mum did not know what to do as my dad was on holiday in Jamaica, and there were no men around to help sort out the situation. Through fear, she let him into the house, to calm him down. She was frightened for my life, but once inside, he appeared to change, and behave normal again, so mum trusted him with me.

When we got to mine, I noticed that the net curtain, which hung at my front door, was torn. Terence in his anger had pushed his hand through the letter box, and ripped it. He was very apologetic for getting so angry, and was nice to me, so I ignored what he had done.

"I love you," he said convincingly. Finally, I could relax.

"Can you make me something to eat?" he asked a while later.

"Yes, let me see to the children first, and put them to bed," I answered.

"Okay," he replied.

Later I handed him a nice plate of steamed fish. His favourite. I watched whilst Terence ate, enjoying my cooking, as always. This pleased me, as I thought things were going to be okay.

"See if the children are sleeping," he suggested after eating.

"Okay." I always did as Terence asked to keep the peace.

"They're fast asleep," I reported.

"Sit down," Terence commanded. His tone of voice had changed.

As I sat down, my heart began to race, as I watched him roll up a newspaper. He marched up and down the living room, then stood over me as I sat on the settee.

"Where were you?" he quizzed aggressively.

"I went to see..." Whack! Terence used the rolled news paper to hit me in the face.

"You're lying," he screamed.

"I'm not." WHACK! Again!

For every time I went to explain to Terence that I went to see my new house, he would smack me in the face.

Suddenly a surge of anger over took me.

"What are you, a detective?" I shouted, getting up from where I was seated.

"How dare you." My words enraged Terence.

Everything went blank. Terence had punched me in my stomach, and smacked my head hard against the wall. I blacked out. After coming round, I gathered myself together but he continued to beat me, jumping on my stomach. Punching and kicking me.

"Please stop," I begged.

After a while, Terence stopped, and began to hug me up as I sobbed my heart out.

"I won't do it again. You made me do it," he claimed.

Giving in to his whims, I lived in the hope that he would someday change and love me in the right way.

Two weeks later, I moved house. Janet moved in around the corner, she lived at 179 and I lived at 173. She now had three children. It was good to have my big sister, living nearby. It made me feel safe. I was scared of Terence, and of the white people in the area. I was in a new environment, and I did not know how my new neighbours would be towards me, being black. In addition, I was now living the other side of Cambridge, far away from my mum and dad. This felt strange; I was so used to having easy access to them.

Janet's back garden overlooked mine, adding to my feeling of security. I could see through one of my back bedroom windows, if there were any cars parked at the front of her house, giving me an idea whether she had visitors or not. I could pop round to see her, if she was on her own. The children could also speak to each other through their bedroom windows. It was fun for them.

About half a mile down the road, lived Sandra, and Dee whose friendship was still closely knitted together with Paula, Susie and Marie. I had not seen any of them for about three years since the day Sandra had come over to my house accusing me and my sisters of talking about her, and her family behind their backs. We had all gone our separate ways, leaving each other to get on with our lives, and this was how I intended to keep it.

CHAPTER 6

WHEN ENOUGH'S ENOUGH

I was pleased to move into my new home. My new neighbours were friendly although there were some racists in the area. 'BLACKIES!' 'NIGGERS!' the words chalked in capital letters, on the pavement outside the shops, stared up at me.

Feeling dismayed, I detached my feelings. There was nothing I could do, but just get on with my life. Racism and fear was not going to get the better of me. I had my children to protect. I wanted to make a go of my life, and make positive changes. I wanted my independence, and not rely on the state to provide for my family. So I went back to work part time as a canteen assistant at the bus company where my dad worked. It was time for me to be responsible. Be a proper mum, and have a routine in place for my children.

With the changes in place, Terence still continued to abuse me. My move had not changed him.

"No-one's gonna want you. You're lucky to have me," he would tease, always putting me down.

His physical and verbal violence towards me, soon took effect. I became obsessive about my household duties, and the hygiene of the children. Everything had to be immaculate, and in its place. I wanted to please him, and feel good about myself, to compensate for his negativity. I would go to bed and remember something I had not done. For example, a handprint on the wall, which I hadn't wiped off; Feeling disturbed I would have to get up, deal with it, then go back to bed. Whenever I had visitors, even for a short time, I would clean the house from top to bottom, dusting, polishing, and hovering as soon as they had gone. I always felt the need to clean. It was my way of shutting out the pain.

Although I was proud of my achievements, I suddenly became overwhelmed with fear. I had a nice clean house adorned with beautiful furniture, and had everything I needed. Yet, if I died, the world was going to carry on, and exist without me. The house would still be standing, people would carry on living, and I would be forgotten.

What could I do to prevent this? How was I going to die? What was it going to be like? Thinking about the thousands, in fact millions of people who had died over the years, I was forced to face the reality of my existence, and the reality of death. As panic made its way into my heart, I felt like solid matter. When I die, my body would disintegrate. Darkness overshadowed me. There was no way out. I was on a journey, in this life, that led to nothing. I had to accept, I did not have the answers. Forcing the thoughts to the back of my mind, I carried on.

Terence and I had been together nearly three years when I became pregnant with my third child. Terence was not pleased. His moods and taunts became more frequent.

"I don't want another baby," he complained.
I did not care; I was going to be responsible for my baby. Terence was not living with me, so he would not have to look after it.

"No-one will want you with children," he continued to taunt.
He would call me names. 'Slut, bitch,' he would shout. Although the abuse was verbal, I would prefer, that he'd hit me. To get it out the way, because his threatening behaviour was like torture.

I would laugh when he laughed, spoke when he spoke, and sat silently when he was silent. I was like Terence's toy, and he was the remote control.

Terence soon became distant towards me. His resentment towards the pregnancy deepened. Fed up of his mood swings, I began to fall out of love with him. He was a bully, and I wanted him to go away.

I had lost all of my friends because he had scared them away. On one occasion he verbally abused my cousin Shirley. He had come to visit me, and I was not at home and not at my parents or sisters', so Terence decided to see if I was at Shirley's. Shirley lived nearby and was going out with someone he knew from Hitchin. Sometimes I would baby-sit for them and she would for us.

"Where is she?" he screamed at Shirley.

"I don't know," Shirley responded in fear. "I'm just babysitting."

I had gone out with someone from work. My work mate had handed in his resignation, and had invited me out for a farewell drink. Because of Terence's attitude, Shirley could not tell him where I was. Disbelieving her, Terence marched to his car and took out a hammer.

"Where is she?" he demanded waving the hammer at Shirley.

"Tell me where she is otherwise I'll smash your house up," he threatened.

"I don't know," Shirley promised, slamming the door in his face.

Terence chopped at the door with the hammer whilst the children began to scream. The police were called. They did not arrest him, but pacified him, and told him to go home.

Arriving back at Shirley's, I could see fear in her face.

"Quick, Quick, get inside, your life's in danger," she exclaimed.

Shirley explained the situation to me.

"Be careful," she warned. "I'm worried for your life. Hide upstairs," Shirley insisted, leading me to a room which belonged to her lodger.

That night I crouched down in the corner of this stranger's room with the children, scared, waiting for the sun to rise, so I could take the children home.

At six in the morning, I made my way home. An hour later the door knocked. Looking through the glass panel I could see Terence's silhouette. Preparing myself for the inevitable, I opened the door. Terence struck me hard across my face.

"You whore. Where have you been?" he demanded.

"I, I" Slap, slap, slap. Terence relieved his temper on my face, not caring, again, about our baby I was carrying.
His reaction added to the feelings of resentment I had towards him.

"Make me some tea," he ordered when he had finally calmed down.

"You're great, you are," he said, kissing me repeatedly all over my face. "I love you," he continued.
Cringing at his words, and touch, my love for Terence was over.

At the end of that year, I had my first premonition. I was lying in bed ready to go to sleep when a surge of fear came over me. I could see Terence shouting at my mum.

He did not care who he insulted, but I knew if he insulted mum, that would definitely be the end of our relationship. I loved my mum very much, and was very close to her. My sisters were always teasing me, saying I was mum's favourite. I wondered whether Terence was secretly jealous of our relationship.

It was New Years Day, when I gave birth to Shekira. She was a very quiet baby, and slept all the time. I was pleased. With two other children to look after, Shekira's quietness made life easy. On the day she was due out of hospital, mum and Terence came to pick us up. As usual, Terence was in a mood, so when we arrived home, kept myself busy, silently pottering around the house, taking down the Christmas decorations, hoping his mood would change.

"Why doesn't she go home?" he hissed at me quietly, referring to mum.

"Leave her alone," I whispered. I did not want mum to hear what he was saying about her.

"All she's doing is sitting down, she should be helping," he sulked.

"Why don't you do something to help, it's your child I've had." Terence did not respond. Mum had entered the Kitchen. Worried and embarrassed I left the kitchen and got on with taking down the Christmas decorations.

"Why don't you go home?" Terence shouted at mum.

"Why should I?" Mum responded.

"You're lazy," he snarled at her and an argument broke out between them.

Mum tried to defend herself. I felt sick in my stomach. It was too much to bear. Running up the stairs crying, Terence chased after me.

"It's over. I've had enough," I screamed.

My premonition had come to pass. Terence had crossed all boundaries now. It was time for me to leave him. The silence could be felt in the air as Terence looked at me with pleading eyes. Holding my head up courageously, looking him in the eyes. My mind was made up.

"Get out," I spoke, without any remorse for him.
Looking down at the floor, Terence left quietly, knowing there was no justification for his actions.

A couple of weeks had passed, and I had not heard from Terence. At last I had peace of mind. No more abuse.

Whilst feeling secure about my new found freedom, Terence appeared.

"I'm sorry, really sorry; I should never have spoken to your mum like that. I've been going through a lot of pressures lately," he explained. "One of my friend's has died, and my uncle was ill," he continued.

I tried my hardest to shut out his words, refusing to take them in. But my heart would not allow me to. It was not in my nature to be unforgiving. Maybe he was stressed. He had many reasons to be. I tried to convince myself.

"I forgive you," I told him after much thought, knowing I did not love him any more.

Reconciling our relationship, Terence and I became an item again. I hoped he had learnt from his behavior, and that this would be a turning point for us. Mum also forgave him, because of me, but said she would never trust him again.

Terence and I did get on much better, but as the children grew older, his lack of parental skills became obvious. He appeared to resent being a father.

"Tell him to sit still," he would say about Rueben.

"Tell her to shut up," he would say about Keisha.

There was no distinction between my child and his. When he came to visit, I noticed the children would go quiet. I would become tense and do my best to make sure they were happy and quiet, in case Terence got upset or irritated.

"I made Michael take his dinner out the bin, and eat it," he boasted one day about his son, from his previous relationship.

"What do you mean?" I questioned, not sure if I was hearing right.

"Yeah, Michael threw his dinner in the bin because he did not want it," he confirmed.

"And you made him take it out, and eat it," I repeated.

"Yep, that's right," Terence confirmed again. He did not care who he abused, adult or child, as long as he was in control.

My birthday was now approaching. Me and Natasha, who was now living back in Cambridge, planned a night out with Terence, and her boyfriend Don. I was delighted at the thought of Natasha being out with me, and Terence. At least he would be nice to me with her being there. On the day of our birthday, Natasha and I got ready at my house.

"What time is Terence coming to pick us up?" she asked.

"Oh, about six o'clock," I replied.

"That's good, that's what time I told Don."

We took our time doing our hair, applying our make-up, and trying on different outfits. I felt so excited to be around Natasha. At exactly six o'clock, Don arrived.

"Terence will be here in a minute," I told him. He was never late. If anything, he was always early.

Six thirty arrived, and there was no sign of Terence.

"I wonder where he is," I thought aloud.

"Maybe he's held up in Traffic," suggested Don, trying to pacify the situation.

At seven o'clock, Terence finally arrived. Happy, I ran to greet him. I was anxious for us to get going. But Terence was in a mood. I decided, I was not going to let his mood spoil my night. It was my day, and I had my twin sister by my side.

"I'll drive us home, so you can have a drink," Don said to Terence. Don's offer lightened his mood. Terence liked to drink.

"Where are we going?" Natasha asked Terence. Terence knew the best places to party. He always knew what was happening for the night.

"We'll go to Luton, to a club where there's a West-Indian restaurant. We'll have something to eat. After that we can go and have a dance," Terence replied.

It took an hour to get to Luton. When we arrived, there was a long queue outside the club. Excited, I couldn't wait to get out the car. I liked seeing long queues; it meant that the night was going to be busy, and lively.

Terence led the way to a restaurant upstairs in the club. The restaurant was well presented with dimmed lights and candles. How romantic!

There were about ten tables clothed with white satin tablecloths, with cutlery and wine glasses set neatly in their place. The smell of curried goat wafted through the air.

"What would you like to eat?" Terence asked, handing me the menu.

"I'll have some curried goat and rice, what about you?"

"Nothing," he replied.

"Nothing? Have something," I insisted gently.

"I said, I don't want anything," he stated aggressively.

Once again, Terence's mood had changed. There was no pleasing him.

"You'll be the only one not eating," Natasha piped in, trying to make light of the situation.

"I'll have some of Fiona's," he sulked.

"Alright," I agreed, disappointedly.

It was unusual for him to share. He loved his West Indian food. Although I wondered what was going through his mind, deep down I knew it was because Natasha was there. He always felt left out when she was around. Being twins, we were so close, making him feel threatened.

After we had finished eating, Natasha suggested we went to the dance area. I agreed, which was unusual for me, without Terence's permission. Later, the men joined us.

I stood around watching whilst everyone danced, and enjoyed themselves. I didn't dare dance myself, because of Terence.

"Hi baby, you look nice," a man whispered in my ear, whilst Terence and Don had gone to the bar.

"Thanks," I answered abruptly. I did not want to be rude, but wanted the man to go away in case Terence saw him talking to me.

"Do you want a dance?" he asked.

"No, go away."

"Come on, let's dance." The man whispered in my ear again, in a sexual way.

"Please go away, my boyfriend will kill me, if he sees you talking to me," I told him.

Grinning from ear to ear, Terence approached from the bar. Though he was smiling I knew he was not happy. The man continued to talk in my ear. Terence pushed my drink angrily in my hand, spilling it over me. He then stormed off. About ten minutes later, he came back. He was composed as though he had put his thoughts into perspective.

At the end of the night we all decided to go to a party at stranger's house. To finish off our birthday.

"Go in with Natasha and Don," Terence insisted.
I found this strange. Terence never let me go anywhere without him. But I did as he told me. It was my birthday. If he wanted to be in a mood, that was his problem.

"Come on," Natasha beckoned me with excitement. "It's packed."

The house was full. You could not move. It was so dark; you could not see where you were going. The music was pumping hard and the smell of marijuana lingered through the air. The warmth of the body heat in the house made me feel safe. And having Natasha with me, made me feel even more safer than ever. Terence could not hurt me.

"Help, no!" a woman amongst the crowd screamed.

"Oh, sorry, wrong person." I could hear Terence's voice. He had attacked this poor lady. He thought she was me.

"Where's the light?" he demanded.

There was a sudden flicker. A man standing next to me had a lighter which he used as a torch.

"Please don't do that, he'll see me," I begged. But it was too late. Terence spotted me.

As he made his way towards me, I prepared my mind for what he was about to do. 'Ouch!' Terence grabbed my breast. The sharp pains seared through me as he dragged me outside through the crowd, holding on as though he was pulling me by my arm. Scared and frightened I began to scream at the passing faces flashing in front of me. Help me! Please help me! I begged. But nobody did. They were scared. Terence was like a vicious animal attacking his prey. In the background, I could hear Natasha pleading on my behalf. But Terence did not listen. He did not care. He continued to humiliate me in front of the crowd of people, who were now outside watching.

"You wanted to see that man from the club," he accused. Terence's jealousy had got the better of him. It was not worth responding to his accusation.

Terence began to punch me repeatedly grabbing hold of my hair, embarrassing me in front of strangers. Natasha and Don became scared too. Terence was like a raging bull. No one dared to approach.

"We're going," he commanded. I believed the beating was over. But I was mistaken!

Crunch! Terence smacked my head against the side of Don's car with all his strength. The pain was unbearable. I thought I was going to die. Pushing me into the back of the car, he gave me another blow to the head with his fist.

"Leave her alone," Natasha screamed.

"I'll leave you here, if you don't leave her alone." Don threatened him. He'd had enough.

Terence went quiet. He knew the only way back to Cambridge was with Don. It was four in the morning and there would be no other way to get home. At home I quietly went to bed and pretended I was asleep. The next day I went straight to mums. Terence went home. Quietly.

A few days later, on his next visit, Terence took his control a step further.

"If you ever have another man in your life, I will use this to kill you," he told me, holding a large axe, which he put on the top of a tall cupboard in the kitchen.

After this incident, I accepted I needed help. My family knew I was being abused by Terence, but did not know to what degree. Natasha was the only person who saw the full extent of what I was going through, but did not know how to help me. We both agreed that it would be difficult for me to leave him, because he would never allow me to. So one day when my little sister suggested we went to a psychic fair, I agreed. I wanted to know my future.

At the psychic fair there were clairvoyants, mediums, crystal ball and tarot card readers. A black man with a large afro, intrigued us. We did not know why, but felt compelled to approach him. We sat in anticipation, as we watched him shuffle the cards, and explain what he was going to do.

"This line represents the past, this one the present, and this, the future," he explained pointing to the cards with strange looking pictures on them.

"Many people hate your third child's father," he said.

"That sounds true!" I exclaimed, enthusiastic to hear more. Although my third child had the same father as my second.

"You're going to drive a black beetle," he went on and on and on. Nothing made sense.

"Can't you tell us something without using the cards?" we asked.

"Yes I can. Wait a minute."

My sister and I waited whilst he held his hands to his head, as though tuning into a radio wave.

"I see a food van. You're selling lots and lots of hotdogs and burgers. You're going to make lots of money. You're also good at art; paint pictures and sell them," he recommended, "You'll make lots of money."

'That's good,' I thought. 'I'm going to be rich.'

Although I felt all he was saying was not true, I held on to what he had said, about everyone hating Terence. At least I had something to cling on to. Everyone, felt the same about Terence, as I did. It wasn't just me.

Shekira was three and a half months old, when Terence dropped the bombshell.

"Come, follow me," he said.

So I followed him, doing as I was told, to the bottom of my road where there was a passage. I was worried, as I thought maybe he was going to kill me, and then dump my body. Looking into the bushes Terence pulled out a plastic bag.

"What's in there?" I asked curiously.

Because Terence did not live in Cambridge, I wondered why he had this bag hidden in a bush, down the bottom of my street.

"Open it when we get back to your place," he replied.

At home I opened the bag, pushed my hand in, and pulled out a pile of cards and love letters. They were from a girl who he had been seeing behind my back for a year. Within the pile, was a picture of her, posing across the bonnet of his car. It was one of the biggest blows of my life. I had stayed with him for four years, depriving myself of having a life, whilst he was entertaining another woman, beating me up, and putting me through mental torture.

"She's pregnant, carrying my child." His stinging words echoed in my head, adding insult to injury.

Speechless and motionless, I needed time to think. Enough was enough. I wasn't prepared to take anymore... I hated him.

CHAPTER 7

WALKING TOWARDS DARKNESS

Terence had now become a thorn in my flesh. He refused to leave me alone. I did not have the strength to stand up to him, so I continued to be with him, knowing, I no longer wanted him, and no longer loved him.

"You're like a brick," he would say, as he tried to cuddle up to me, sensing how I was feeling.

"You love her more than me," he would accuse about Shekira.

He had become jealous of his own child. This made me more anxious to get rid of him. So when feelings began to arise in my heart for someone else, I began to rebel against Terence and his strict regime and control over me.

I was at Janet's when Nigel walked in.

"Hi," I pouted, as Janet introduced him to me. Looking Nigel up and down, I had an immediate desire to be with him.

"Hello," he responded in clear spoken English.

I had never heard a black man speak like that before. Usually they spoke patois, (Jamaican). But Nigel was different. His eloquence was attractive to me.

"How do you know him?" I questioned Janet, following her through the sitting room door, into the hallway of her house.

"Who?" Janet questioned back.

"Nigel, he's lovely."

"You can't have him."

"Why?"

"Because he goes out with Shirley. She doesn't want anyone to know, because she's just finished with her boyfriend."

Nigel did not leave my mind. He was tall dark and handsome with dominant black features. He had big lips and lovely big eyes. He had long eyelashes with thick jet black eyebrows. He had broad shoulders, and stood upright with great confidence. Nigel wore designer clothes. The best you could find. He was very charming, well mannered, and intellectual. I believed he was a sensible person. I was more drawn to him, when Janet and Shirley, told me about a tablet, that Nigel and his friend Martin, had given to them. The tablet sounded like the remedy I needed to help me feel good about myself.

"You should try one," Janet had said. "It keeps you awake all night and makes you feel like a woman."

"And they make you feel confident," Shirley continued.
The curiosity about this tablet played on my mind; 'I must try one when I get the opportunity,' I thought.

It was a quiet afternoon, a week after meeting Nigel; as usual I was in the house waiting in case Terence turned up. I was bored so I began to read the daily newspaper from cover to cover, to pass the time away. Engrossed in what I was doing, I suddenly heard a tap on the sitting room window. It was Nigel. 'What was he doing here? What if Terence turns up and sees him. I'll be in serious trouble.'

"Hi, open the door," he gestured pointing to the front door.

Nigel's face was beaming as he grinned at me. How could I resist. Prince charming had come to rescue me. Terence flashed through my mind once again. 'Oh well, I don't care', I convinced myself, as I rushed with excitement to open the front door.

"Hello," I smiled as I opened the door.

"You all right?" he responded still smiling.

"So, are you going to let me in?" he asked.

"Oh!" My mind had drifted, staring into his face. "Quickly come in, my boyfriend might turn up," I told him.

I quickly ushered him into the house. I did not want anyone to see him coming in. I made a plan in my mind; if Terence turned up I would hide Nigel in the cupboard under the stairs.

Explaining to Nigel about Terence, I told him, he could only stay for a few minutes.

"I'm not scared of him," he claimed.

"I am."

"I can handle him," he continued.

"Why have you come here?"

"I've come to see you."

"Well, I don't think its right, because you go out with Shirley, and she's my cousin."

"Shirley? We're only having a bit of fun. It's nothing serious," Nigel promised.

We continued to talk about anything and everything. I did not say I liked him and he did not say he liked me although the chemistry was there. If Nigel had made an advance towards me, I knew I would be unable to resist. After about an hour, Nigel left.

Later that day Terence arrived. My hatred for him became stronger. Especially now I had the attention of another man. As Terence tried to kiss me, I pushed him away. Storming off to the kitchen, he took out the axe.

"Don't forget, this is for you," he reminded me.

"What have I ever done to you?" I questioned, fearfully.

Terence knew time was running out for him. He had done me too many wrongs. For me there was no hope of reconciliation. His bad ways far outweighed any good that was in him.

Shirley soon confided, that her and Nigel were seeing each other. But I did not bargain on what she was about to say.

"He fancies you," Shirley hissed.

"Who?" I asked, knowing full well who she meant.

"Nigel," she replied with a half raised voice. I could hear the hurt in her tone.

"What did he say?"

"Nothing, I just know he does, but I don't blame you, it's him. You're feeling vulnerable."

She obviously liked Nigel more than she was letting on, and I did not want to hurt her. So I decided to leave things alone and put my feelings for him aside.

On Terence's next visit, I had made up my mind. It was time to confront him, and tell him the truth. I could no longer pretend to love him. So I told him it was over between us, and that I never wanted to see him again except in regards to the children. Terence pleaded and pleaded. Despite seeing the pain and hurt in his eyes, I felt no remorse.

"I need time to think," I lied, so that he would leave me alone.

"Let's not see each other for a week," I continued.
Terence agreed. He was now under my control.
Shirley and Nigel also ended their relationship. I was secretly pleased, and convinced myself that it would be okay to go on a date with Nigel, as they had only been together for three weeks. So I devised a plan. Looking through my bedroom window, I waited for his car to pull up outside Janet's house, and when it did, I went round pretending to visit. Terence would not be visiting for a whole week. I had to act fast!

On visiting Janet's, Nigel was not there but his friend Martin was. He had borrowed Nigel's car to visit Janet. 'I could ask him what he thought about me getting with Nigel',

I thought. But there was one problem. Martin was Sandra's boyfriend. Although she lived in the area, I had not seen her. I did not want any involvement with her or anything to do with her life. 'I'll play it safe,' I thought. I wanted Nigel and now had the opportunity to get him.

"I like your friend," I nervously told Martin, as he leaned against the kitchen shelf.

"Who, Nigel?" he asked.

"Yes, do you think he would like me?" I questioned.

"I don't know," Martin answered, looking at me curiously.

"I tell you what, why don't you arrange for me, you and Nigel to go out together, tonight for a drink?" I suggested boldly.

"Alright," Martin smirked. Suspicious of my request.

"I'll pick you up at eight o'clock. Be ready."

I eagerly rushed home. I could not believe I had taken the courage to arrange something like this. Something that would change the course of my life. Enough was enough. Terence was no longer my master.

That night, Martin picked me up at eight o'clock as arranged. My plan had worked so far. Nigel was with him.

"Where do you want to go?" Martin asked me.

"Anywhere, I don't mind."

As long as I could get with Nigel, I did not care where I went. I knew I was playing a dangerous game, with Terence in the background. I had gone past caring. My heart was dead towards him, and alive for Nigel.

"What's this music?" I enquired, amused, as we travelled through the Cambridge roads, at forty miles an hour, in a thirty miles an hour speed zone. I had never heard this type of music before, and did not like the sound of it, although Nigel and Martin appeared to really enjoy it.

"It's called 'house music,'" replied Nigel.
Charmed by the sound of his voice, my stomach began to do somersaults.

"House? I've never heard of this before."
This music was strikingly different from the reggae music I was used to. It was very strange!

We arrived at our destination, a pub, in a country part of Cambridge. The unfamiliarity of where I was, brought me back to my senses. There I was, with two men I hardly knew in the middle of nowhere. What was I doing? What was I thinking? My confidence suddenly left me and I began to feel uncomfortable, until I remembered the tablets. 'They make you feel like a woman,' I could hear Janet saying. 'They give you confidence,' Shirley had said.

Boldly, I asked, "can I have one of your tablets?"

"What tablets?" Nigel inquired innocently, as though he did not know what I was talking about.

"There's a tablet that you take and it makes you feel good; what is it called?" I asked.
Nigel and Martin looked at each other. I could see by their expressions, they were in serious thought.

"Well, I don't know if you'll handle it," Nigel finally responded.

"I don't care. Let me try one. I can handle anything," I insisted.

"Alright, but be careful," Martin advised as he handed me the tablet.

"After about fifteen minutes, you'll get a sudden rush," he informed me.

Quickly swallowing the tablet, I couldn't wait for it to work. Martin was not wrong. Fifteen minutes later the rush went through my veins like hot coals of fire, as I became detached from reality. I had entered a new world. A world of peace and love. My confidence came back. I felt like a woman just like Janet and Shirley had said I would.

Nigel and Martin were very popular. Their phones rang constantly.

"We'll be there in a minute," I would hear them say.

We soon left the pub and they made several stops without staying too long.

"Why are you stopping at all these places?" I asked.

"Oh everyone wants some of these tablets."

"Gosh, they must be popular."

"Yeah, they cost fifteen pounds each, so we make lots of money from them," Martin informed me.

"That's good," I replied not thinking the tablets were dangerous, and not realising they were big time drug dealers.

Some of the people whom they dropped the tablets to, were people I knew. There was a different world in my community, which I did not know existed. A world, I was to find, of darkness, void, and falseness.

As the night continued, I craved to show Nigel how much I liked him, so on our way home; I invited him back to my place. Nigel was more than happy. As my body desired his, the control of the drugs, held no barriers. Surrendering to Nigel's touch, my ties with Terence were broken. At last, I was safe from the brute that had been ruling my live.

The night was over quickly and daylight soon arrived. The effects of the tablet had now worn off and the truth of the matter was in front of me.

"I've made a mistake; I've behaved like a slut," I said. Sobbing my heart out, I told Nigel to go.

"You're not a slut," he comforted, wrapping his arms around me.

"Please don't tell anyone what's happened between us," I cried. "They'll think badly of me."
Reassuring me, Nigel agreed that he would not tell anyone.

I convinced myself, the whole night was a dream. It was not really me. It was someone else inside of me. I had behaved with false confidence, looking for something to make me feel better about my life and myself. The tablet had worked for a few hours, but not anymore. I had to face what was before me, and put an end to me and Terence.

During that week whilst waiting for Terence to arrive, Nigel and I spent every evening together. I felt secure. The children welcomed him, and Nigel them. He bought Rueben a spinning top, and helped with the girls. He promised he would look after me once I had dealt with Terence. Reassured and elated, I believed him.

"You speak very good English," I told Nigel.

"I'm adopted," he confessed. "I was brought up to speak this way. My parents are white. Mum's German and my dad's American, and a professor," he added. "They adopted me in America."

I became more intrigued by Nigel. A black man brought up by white parents. Speaking English, and not the Jamaican patois, I was used to. He lived a different lifestyle, to what I was used to. A lifestyle I never knew existed.

"What about my children? Have you got any?"
Sharing my fears with Nigel, I was not sure whether he would be able to take me on with three young children. Also he was a couple of years younger than me. I was twenty four and he was twenty one. I wondered whether he would be able to cope with us.

"I don't have any, but it's okay, I love children." He told me.
It was true Nigel did love children. He had already proved it to me. In the few days we'd been together, he had changed Shekira's nappies, and made her bottles. He played with Rueben and Keisha accepting her tantrums. He was great with all of them.

Friday arrived and Terence was due to turn up on the Sunday, and I was scared. Nigel and I had become close, and he was determined to stand by me.

"I don't want his dirty hands on you." He reassured, making me feel special.

"He'll kill me. That's why he's got the axe on the top of the cupboard. I don't think you understand. I'll have to get a court injunction out against him, so that he cannot hurt me."

Nigel understood, and did not leave my side. We spent the day walking through town, going from solicitor to solicitor, trying to get a court injunction against Terence. It was Friday and we had to make sure we got one that day. The solicitors would be closed over the weekend. But we had no success, so I resigned myself, to face whatever was to come.

We'd just had Sunday dinner, when Terence walked through the back door, which led into the kitchen. Nigel was in there. He was in the process of lighting a spliff off the cooker. He was a great smoker of marijuana and was very much addicted to it. I was standing in the hallway. I could feel my legs giving up on me, as I trembled with fear. Terence looked lost. He did not question why Nigel was in the house. He had obviously weakened, and accepted the fact, that he had lost control over me.

"Go in there," I said, to Terence, pointing to the sitting room door, wanting him out the way.

Once he entered the sitting room, I exited through the front door and began to run, making my way to Janet's house.

"Fiona," Terence called, chasing after me.

"Murder, murder," I screamed in mums face. Thank God she was at Janet's. Mum's presence would hopefully calm the situation down a bit, and soften the blows that were to come.

"What is it?" Mum's expression showed her fear.
Seeing Terence behind me, mum knew I was in a panic about him. She did not know what I had been up to with Nigel. If I had told her; she would never have allowed it. Calming me down, mum addressed Terence.

"Terence what's going on?"

"She's been seeing someone else," he told her.

"No I haven't," I denied.
Mum looked at me raising her eyebrows. Terence was possessive. Because of this, mum believed me.

"Let's talk about things here," I suggested to Terence, pleading with him not to be violent in Janet's house.
Agreeing with me, we went into one of Janet's rooms for privacy, where he asked me the inevitable.

"Are you seeing him?"
My heart racing, I decided to tell Terence the truth. I was safe in my sister's house. Besides Nigel would protect me. He was my man now and I was his woman. As far as I was concerned, Terence and I were buried long ago.

Terence was unusually calm. I'd never seen him like this before. Maybe he had given in, accepting it was too late to react.

"I'll leave you alone, but I want to know, when can I see the children?"

"Once a week on a Saturday," I quickly suggested.

Terence agreed without a fuss. I now had back, full control of my life. The ball was in my court. I was in charge. I was free. We continued to talk and discussed the issues of the children. Feeling relaxed that everything was going to be alright, Terence asked the dreaded question.

"Have you slept with him?"

His eyes were pierced with anger, and with pain. His lips pursed tight and his jaw crunched together, as though he was gritting his teeth. Hesitating, the question went over and over in my mind. Finally I answered.

"No," I lied.

I wanted to say yes. But couldn't. I remembered the axe, his words and his past. Terence would not hesitate to use it.

"I want to speak to Nigel alone," he announced after leering at me.

Terence knew I was not telling him the truth.

"I want to make sure he doesn't hurt the children. I'll go back to yours and talk to him there."

Uneasy about Terence's request, I followed him after a few minutes. I did not trust his plea.

Martin and another of their friend's had arrived. They sat in a car parked outside the house watching Nigel and Terence. They were in conversation at the side of the house beside the back door. As I approached them, Terence's face told a story. He was not happy.

"Let's go inside," Terence suggested.

"That's fine," Nigel answered smugly.

Nigel's strength and courage towards Terence enhanced my feelings for him. He was willing to protect me. Be a man and stand up for me.

Nigel's friend's continued to wait outside whilst we went in. Entering the sitting room, I sat down comfortably on the settee, thinking they were going to sit down too. But both men remained standing, staring each other in the eyes. Looking up at them, I felt small from where I was sitting. Continuing to stare into Nigel's face, Terence shut the living room door, guarding it by pushing his hand against it, so we were tightly compacted without any escape.

"Fiona, have you slept with him?" Terence asked again.

"No," I lied again.

"He says you have," Terence beckoned to Nigel.

Laughing nervously, like a child, I peeped up at Nigel to get a response. I could tell he had told him. He was claiming me as his woman.

Terence's hand came down on me with force, as he struck me hard across the face. I could see stars, as the light in the room turned to darkness. Feeling embarrassed in front of Nigel, I quickly tried to compose myself. My laughter turned into shame. The blackness took a few moments to disappear. Coming to my senses, I could see Nigel's hand's around Terence's neck. Jumping up, I hesitantly watched as Nigel threw Terence down by the throat onto the settee. Careering across the room on the settee, Nigel was on top of Terence. Looking for a way out, I spotted the door. I ran down the road to Janet's, again screaming murder; I needed to call the police. I was convinced someone was going to be killed.

Whilst I was gone, Terence had grabbed a knife to stab Nigel. Fortunately for Nigel his mates were still outside. They ran in the house when they saw the state I was in. Terence had dropped the knife as soon as he saw them. He broke down and cried. He was backed into a corner. There was nothing he could do. His time of reigning was over.

The police arrived and cautioned Terence. They warned him to stay away. They did not see the need to arrest anyone, because it was a domestic situation. No one was hurt.

"I just want to say one more thing to her before I go," Terence pleaded with the police.

"Alright," they agreed.

With the police guarding my side, Terence got down on his knees.

"Will you marry me?" He proposed.

'How dare he think I would turn back now? Give him power over me again!' I knew this was Terence's way to try and get my attention. Most women like the thought of marriage. Maybe I would have married him before. But not now. I despised him. Not just for the violence but also for the deceit.

"Come on, leave now," the Police ordered him.

Terence left crying with his head hanging low, sad and defeated.

After several attempts to get me back, Terence threatened to burn the house down. Eventually he had a mental breakdown. Once he crawled around the floor on his hands and knees in a state of confusion, saying 'what am I going to do.' And at times he would head butt the walls. He then tried to kill himself by taking an overdose of tablets. He was so unstable, he escaped from hospital, but the police found him and took him back.

"What's wrong with me?" he told me, he'd asked the doctor.

"The woman you love, has walked out on you. You are suffering from a broken heart," he said the doctor had diagnosed.

Terence finally left me alone when he accepted I was in love with Nigel. I did not see him again until years later.

CHAPTER 8

LOOKING FOR ANSWERS

Nigel moved in with me straight away, changing my lifestyle, and the way I did things, almost instantly. Instead of cooking the West Indian dishes that I was so used to, I began to cook the fast foods which Nigel loved. Burgers, chips, and anything greasy. My routine for my children also changed, as I tried to keep up with Nigel's late nights, and lay-ins. He never got up before one or two o'clock in the afternoon, and would expect me to stay in bed with him.

"Just stay a little while longer," he would entice. With the warmth of his body, and the security of his touch, I would surrender to his suggestion.

I would quickly sort out the children by giving them their breakfast. Then leave them, to either play with their toys in their bedroom, or sit them downstairs in front of the TV. By the time I did get up, they would be desperate for my attention.

It was very hard fitting into this new world that Nigel had introduced me to. It was out of the norm for me. Because of his background, most of his friends were white English. They all spoke the same dialect, and liked 'this house music' that I greatly despised. This music, to me, sounded like something out of star trek.

"This is how you dance to it." Nigel showed me one day, as he hopped around my living room, moving his hands in the air.

Nigel could see I was unimpressed by what he was doing, but promised I would enjoy it, when he took me out to a rave at the weekend.

Walking across a large field, wearing high heels and mini skirt, I knew I'd made a mistake.

"Where are we going?" It was pitch black and we were in the middle of nowhere.

"To a warehouse."

'A warehouse!' he must me joking. As I looked up, I realised this was no joke. I could hear the music pumping loudly, like police sirens in an emergency.

Entering the warehouse I noticed that everyone looked the same. The men had cropped hair, (shaped like washing up bowls), with partings down the middle. Whereas the women had theirs crunched in a bun on the top of their heads. Most wore baggy jumpers; baggy jeans, trainers and they all did the same dance. The dance that Nigel had shown me. I spotted a couple of black faces amongst the crowd. They dressed and danced just like everyone else. This was bizarre to me. Although there had been a rise in the black population in Cambridge, I would never have thought they would be into this kind of thing. I always had the belief that all, black people only mixed in our own culture, and would not adopt any other.

Conscious of my appearance, I wished the floor would swallow me up.

"Where do they get all their energy from?" I asked Nigel, as I watched everyone dancing at a very fast pace.

"By taking those tablets," Nigel explained. "Do you want one?"

"What are they called?" Until this time I did not know what they were.

"Ecstasy," he told me. "They come in different strengths. These ones are really strong. They make you feel great." Nigel convinced me.

I did not really want to take one because of the affect it would have on me the next day. But because I believed it would boost my confidence, like the last time, and get me through the night, I quickly swallowed the tablet.

Ten minutes later, I felt the sudden rush again. This time, it did not have the same impact on me. I was too aware of my appearance, and as the paranoia set in, I wanted to go home. I did not belong in this new world. I would never fit in.

With bright lights streaming through the air, the people looked like zombies. This world was unreal. I yearned for my reggae music, and the comfort of my local pub and friends. I was lost. But it was too late to turn back now. My emotions were tied up with Nigel. I was already hooked on him.

We had been together a few weeks, when Nigel's attitude towards me changed. He began to do as he pleased, without a care for my feelings. He would go off to different places; one minute he was at a friend's house, the next minute in a pub, then the next minute in a club. He would pop home to see me during the day, and would go be out most the night. Without me!

"Where are you going tonight?" I would ask.

"I don't know," he would reply.

"Can I come?"

"No." This would be is answer every time.

"What time shall I expect you back then?"

"Dunno."

Nigel behaved shiftily every time I confronted him. He would never look me in the eyes. Whenever I asked him any questions, he would get agitated. I was embarrassed in front of my family by the way he was treating me. 'Had I made a mistake leaving Terence?' I questioned myself.

"You've jumped out of the frying pan into the fire," my dad affirmed.

Dad's remark stirred up something inside of me. My inner being wanted to prove to every one that I had not made a mistake... Nigel was a good person, and at least not as bad as Terence.

Nigel soon disappeared, and never came home. No one knew where he was. As a couple of days turned into a week, my instincts began to speak to me. 'He's seeing Samantha,' I thought. I had known Samantha years ago; she was my first boyfriend's sister! I had seen her talking to him in the Portland Arms one night. Nigel told me she was getting some drugs from him. Although I was not convinced, I believed him. I had no proof that he was lying.

After a week and a half, in the middle of the night, Nigel finally turned up. He was casual about his behaviour. He had no explanation, and was not apologetic. I expected, especially after his fight with Terence, that he would make an extra effort to make things work with me. Wrapping his arms around me, Nigel whispered,

"I love you."

Feeling secure, I went to sleep believing he would tell me where he had been in the morning.

"I want to have fun," Nigel explained, as I opened my eyes. "I'm not ready to give you what you want." He continued.

My heart sinking, I could not believe what I was hearing.

"So what are you saying?" I needed to know, what did having fun mean to Nigel.

"We could get back together later," Nigel concluded, confirming what I feared. He did not want to be with me anymore.

Pretending that I understood he was young and needed to experience life, I asked him a question, dreading the answer. My instincts were still speaking to me.

"Can I just ask you something?... Are you seeing Samantha?"

Nigel went quiet. Turning to me, he spoke in a soft voice. Hearing the word 'Yes,' felt like a knife had been plunged through my heart. My instincts were right. I was betrayed again, by another woman.

After he left, pride entered my heart. Samantha was not going to have him. How could she do this to me! She was a pretty girl in her early thirties who I always looked up to. She kept herself to herself, and had gone away to live in America with her husband several years ago. She was now back in Cambridge to live. It was obvious that she had taken a wrong turn in her life, as she was now taking cocaine and ecstasy. Samantha was disappointed at the failure of her marriage, and now I was a victim of this breakdown.

I was determined to get Nigel back. I was not going to allow anyone to put me to shame. Moreover, I had to prove to my family, and my friends that I had not made a mistake. Nigel did love me.

Looking to Janet for support, she introduced me to some new male friends of hers. She had changed. She was usually a quiet person. She had never kept company with certain types of people until now. Her new friends took drugs. They mixed with both the black and white community. They gave me a deeper insight into house music and the English culture. One of them was Craig. I had known of him, from my upbringing in the black community. He was a gentle guy who spoke a lot about the spiritual world which intrigued us all. He seemed to seek spirits to get comfort in his times of need. He was lost and lonely, and desperate for love. My sister had become a rock to him.

Craig knew Nigel and Martin very well. He would get supplies of drugs from them for everyone. Speed, ecstasy, weed, acid tabs and cocaine.

We all began to spend many days and nights looking for answers from the spiritual books, which I had introduced them to. I did card readings, and we all did the oracles in desperation. I hadn't seen Nigel for a while. I needed to know why he preferred Samantha to me. 'What was different about her?' 'Was he ever going to come back to me?' But none of these oracles gave me the answers that I wanted.

"You're going to lose all your possessions, bit by bit," Janet said to me, after doing one of the oracles.

"No I'm not." I was defiant, that this was not going to happen. But somewhere in my heart, I felt that this was going to be true, but brushed this thought to the back of my mind.

A month went past, there was still no sign of Nigel, so Craig suggested I spoke to Sandra about him. Her boyfriend, Martin had cheated on her with her best friend, who was Samantha's sister! So we both had something in common. Nigel and Martin had cheated on us with two sisters, and we both wanted them back. My dad always said, 'never look back. Keep going forward.' But I could not resist the temptation. I wanted to know about Nigel. Hopefully, I agreed to meet up with Sandra.

Six years had passed since I had last seen her. She appeared to be a different person to how she used to be. She had kept up her adoption of the Rastafarian faith and way of living. She was adorned with long dreadlocks which reached down to the bottom of her back. She wore long skirts down to her ankles, and always wrapped the front of her hair. She was now a mother of five children. Sandra was well into the bible, and spoke with great faith. She appeared to have a lot of wisdom and knowledge. Her words of advice were very comforting. Everyone seeked her assistance whenever they were troubled.

"Nigel and Martin are habitual," she told me.

"What does that mean?" I asked.

"They like their family homes. Even though they're out there doing what they want, they see us as their wives." She claimed. "They'll be back," Sandra reassured me.

This made me feel good. It was only a matter of time before I would win Nigel back. Sandra knew Nigel a bit more than I did due to his friendship with Martin, whom she had been with for years. She said Nigel was like a brother to her, so when she said that he liked me, I believed her.

"Let's promise to always be honest with each other, never hiding anything. That way we'll avoid any bad feelings," I suggested to Sandra.

We were getting close. I had begun to look up to her, and admired her. She needed me, and I needed her, but I did not want history to repeat itself. I put our past, down to that fact we were all young at that time, so all could now be forgiven. I meant it from my heart.

"That's fine by me," Sandra agreed.

With our pact in place, Sandra introduced me personally to her white friends. Dee, Paula, Marie and Susie. Although I knew them from the past, I did not know them personally. I was amazed when I discovered they all liked this house music, smoked a lot of weed, and enjoyed taking ecstasy and speed. They said they had been into this way of living for a long time.

"How did you get into all this?" I asked them.

"Well, me, and Paula were in London one night looking for a reggae do to go to. We were walking past a club and we heard this loud music playing. It sounded really lively. 'Let's go in, Paula had said,' so I agreed. We took an ecstasy tablet, and never looked back since." Susie explained.

Sandra and I were soon spending a lot of time together. We would stay up late, talking about Nigel and Martin, and the girls they had gone off with. Sometimes we would be at Janet's, with her friends. My children soon took second place again. I tended to them when necessary, but that was it. Because of the late nights I became exhausted, finding it hard to cope with my daily household chores. I had also started to smoke more and more weed, and would take ecstasy nearly every night. I lived in a bubble. I needed something to fill the void in my heart. Terence's abuse and Nigel's rejection had left me feeling empty and lonely.

Every time Craig went to see Nigel and Martin, to get some ecstasy tablets, Sandra and I would question him. 'What were they doing? Where were they going? Were they with them? Did they mention us?' We were obsessed with them, and their relationships with these girls.

"They're all going out tonight," Craig would report.

"Samantha and Nigel have had an argument," he would say. I was always aware of what was going on.

On the few occasions that I bumped into Nigel at Sandra's house, I would always be nice to him, hoping to get into his good books... waiting for the time, when he would come back me.

Looking for comfort, in the taking of ecstasy, and the reading of cards, soon wore off. We were getting no answers by having a buzz at night, and being abnormal all day. Our next hope was seeking help from the spiritual world. Anxious to know what was going to happen to me, I needed answers. Sandra had spoken of different spirits, good and bad, which she had come up against.

"I tell them to get lost if they're bad. I'm not scared of them," she had said.

We were at Janet's house looking through the spiritual books, to see if there was anything else we could do when Janet spotted it.

"Let's do a séance," she suggested.

I had heard stories in the past of how séances worked, and was always intrigued. People would call upon the spirits of the dead. They would get answers for their problems.

Janet's idea appeared to be a breakthrough for me. I would know what was going to happen in the future.

"Come on let's do it," Craig urged with excitement. "I know what to do," he continued.

I watched carefully whilst he cut up twenty-six small squares of paper. On each square, he wrote a letter of the alphabet.

He put the squares in alphabetical order in a circle around the edges of the table.

"We need a glass to put in the middle of the circle," he told us.

Janet quickly fetched one. We all silently took our places around the table, watching in anticipation, as Craig placed the glass down gently.

"Right, we all have to put our hands on the glass."

We all did as we were told.

"Is anybody there?" Craig asked, speaking into the air.

There was no response. So he asked again.

"Is anybody there?"

Still no response.

"I don't feel right doing this." One of Janet's friends moaned.

"I tell you what; let me and Craig do it," I suggested. I was too excited to stop this process.

After much discussion and debate, it was agreed that it was best for Craig and I to do it together, as we believed in it.

"Is anybody there?" we asked together.

There was a slight pause then a screeching noise as the glass slid slowly across the table to the Y. I looked at Craig and he looked at me. He knew and I knew that we did not move the glass.

"Is anybody there?" Craig continued.

This time the glass glided to the letters 'e' and, 's' spelling 'yes'. At this point, I felt at ease. We were getting somewhere.

"Who are you?" Craig asked.

With his lips clenched and eyes widened, I wondered what Craig was seeing. Unexpectedly I felt as though something had entered into me.

"No!" I screamed grabbing hold of Janet's wrist.

Pushing past everyone I ran up the stairs. Thud, thud, thud, everyone followed me trampling like a herd of elephants except Craig. We were all scared of him. Craig looked like a completely different person. His expressions were serious, and his posture became upright like someone in authority.

"Come back," he bellowed in a loud voice, which sounded like a roar.

Peering over the banister of the stairs, neither of us wanted to go near him. We were afraid of what he might do. The situation eventually calmed down when Craig was back to himself.

"Look at my wrist," Janet showed us.

Her wrist was swollen with welt marks.

"What happened?" we all asked.

"Fiona did it when she grabbed hold of me."

"No I didn't!" I said, surprised that I could possibly have done such a thing to her.

My strength alone could not possibly of done it.

"Shall I tell you what word came to me when I asked who was it?" Craig asked us.

"What word?" We all asked waiting in suspense.

"Beelzebub."

"Who's that?" I asked.

"The devil."

As soon as the words left his lips, I knew the devil was something bad. I knew there was a spiritual world, but had never heard of anything bad like this. From the stories I had heard from my childhood, I always believed that the spiritual world was all good. The mark on Janet's arm spoke for itself; we were all now terrified because of what we had done. We had called up a bad spirit, and hoped it would now go away.

"What are we going to do?" Janet pleaded. "This has happened in my house. I'm worried for my safety."

"Burn the bits of papers and throw them outside," suggested Craig. "The spirit will then leave."

And this is what was done. We burnt the bits of papers with the letters on, and threw them outside.

That night we all slept in the same bed. Before going to sleep, we drew crosses above our beds knowing that this would protect us. We knew there was power in the cross. We believed it could overcome all evil.

The next night I was still spooked up. I had always been scared of the dark, and now it was made worse.

"Will you stay on my sofa tonight?" I begged Mark, one of Janet's friends. "I'm really frightened." I pleaded.

Mark agreed. Whilst he settled down on my settee, I went to bed. Lying in bed, I could hear Mark playing the stereo downstairs at full volume. Frustrated by the noise, I began to call out to Mark.

"M a r k, M a r k." Struggling to speak, no sound was coming from my mouth. A heavy weight was pressing down on me, paralysing me so I could not move.

"M a r k, M a r k." I called. This time my voice was hoarse.

"M a r k, M a r k." I tried to call again, managing to drag myself across to the edge of the bed.

Trying to move my body, I could feel this thing dragging me back. The presence of this thing was dark. Remembering the word Beelzebub, and what had happened to Janet, I became frightened for my life. I was terrified!

Determined to be set free from this thing I fought back. Grabbing hold of my bed covers as tightly as possible, I was suddenly released. Rushing down the stairs, I met with Mark, who was sound asleep!

"Wake up, wake up." I shrieked.

"What's wrong?" Mark asked puzzled by my anxiety.

"Did you have the music on?"

"No." He said.

"Are you sure, I heard it. It was really loud."

"I went straight to sleep when you went upstairs." He explained.

Mark was oblivious to what had gone on.

After this episode, we all had problems. Pictures were moved around. Items went missing. I also had problems getting to sleep. The spirit we had awoken, would not leave us alone. We had opened the door to let it in. We did not know how to shut it.

It was three o'clock in the morning, another late night sitting up with Janet and her friends; when Janet started to behave, as though she was someone else.

"I don't feel like me," she told us.
Janet looked grey. She was shaking.

"What's the matter? You do seem different," I stated.

"I don't know. I just feel strange, like something is inside of me. I don't like it."

About an hour later, Janet started to look even greyer. She said, she was feeling more and more different by the minute. She began to rock to and fro, and said she felt like she was a prostitute and that there was a violent streak in her.

"I don't like me. I feel like I could hurt someone," she explained.

"We need to do something," Craig suggested. "Let's take her to Sandra's. She knows about the spiritual world."

"That's a good idea," we all agreed.
The morning air was cold and frosty, so we hurriedly crammed ourselves into Craig's mini, heading with hope, to Sandra's house to get rid of this spirit.

On the way to Sandra's, the atmosphere changed. There was a definite, cold smoky presence in the car, that was unexplainable;

"It feels like someone's in the car with us," Craig dared to say.

"Uhm." Speechless through apprehension, this was the only response I could give.

We all sensed the same thing. It was now in the car, with us.

"Help!" Janet screamed.

Trying not to panic for the sake of Janet... I began to pray, that we would get through this awful situation, and that Sandra would deliver us from this evil.

Sandra greeted us with a smile. Fortunately, she was still up.

"Something's come in with you," she told us.

"Can you feel it?" Asked Craig anxiously. He was relieved that Sandra, could sense something was wrong. It meant our luck was in. We explained to her what we had done, and what had been happening.

"Come on," Sandra said to Janet, ushering her into her living room gently. Janet was now sobbing uncontrollably.

Picking up her bible, Sandra began to scream loudly, with all her might, at the spirit.

"Get lost," she shouted. "Go away."

She then began to swear at it.

"Go away, get out," she commanded.

She then stormed up and down the stairs, into her front room, into her kitchen then back into the sitting room, where we all sat rooted to the settee, waiting for an end to this horrible situation. Gradually we felt the presence lifting until it eventually disappeared. Sandra became our heroine. I believed she had released us from the power of darkness.

After this experience, we never did a séance again. As far as I was concerned, I'd had a lucky escape. I put an end to the late nights, and regained my routine with the kids. After all, Shekira was still a baby. She needed my undivided attention. Giving my house a big clear out, and a spring clean, I put myself back on track.

CHAPTER 9

THE PIPE!

Although my life calmed down, my heart was still set on Nigel. Autumn was in season. The long days and cold nights, added to my loneliness. So when there was an unexpected knock on the door, I welcomed the unexpected visitor. Smoothing my hair, and checking that the clothes I was wearing were neat and in place, I hurried, my heart beating fast, sweating nervously, to open the door.

"Hello," I greeted my visitor. Six years had passed, and there was Oliver standing at my door.

'Thank God', I was glad that he had come at a time when my life was organised. Otherwise, he might have had something to say.

"Hello," Oliver responded with his smooth voice, raising one of his eyebrows, reminding me of the past that was long gone. His demeanour left me with no choice but to welcome him in.

"How did you know where to find me?" I questioned him.

"I went to the Portland Tavern and saw Shirley and she told me where you lived."

In a daze, I wondered what else Shirley had told him. Did she mention me and Nigel and all the mix up?

"So you've come to see Rueben at last." I did not know what to make of Oliver's visit.

"Of course!" he said.

Still numb to the pains of the past, I carried on as though nothing had happened.

Rueben was pleased to see Oliver. His face beaming with joy, he welcomed Oliver with open arms. I had told him so much about Oliver. I explained that he had to go away to Germany, because he was in the army, and that he would come back one day. I did not tell him the whole truth of the matter. I did not want to break his heart and make him feel abandoned. We all spent the afternoon laughing, joking, breaking down all barriers. Oliver was impressed with my home, the way I was as a mother, and the quality of the children's clothes.

"You've done well," he complemented. "You're cooking's nice too," he commented after dinner. It was as though we were the family that we should have been.

"I'm surprised you're friends with her." Oliver caught my attention.

"Who?"

"Sandra." Oliver had obviously done his homework.

"Why?" I was now hoping Oliver would tell me the truth about his relationship with Sandra. His remark had dug up what I had buried in my heart.

"Oh nothing," he replied casually as if to brush me off. But his answer did not satisfy me.

"Did you sleep with her?" I was now comfortable with Oliver, and believed he would confess to his actions of the past. Although I had made friends with Sandra, Oliver's statement opened a door in my heart that I had shut. Hearing the truth from him would enable me to put this ghost to rest, once and for all.

Oliver sat quietly. His perplexed appearance showed, he was in deep thought. After a short while the word spat out of his mouth.

"No," he answered unconvincingly.

"You're lying," I accused. "Admit it."

He refused to admit what had happened. Instead he casually diverted the subject back to Rueben.

"Can I take Rueben to London with me for the night? I'll introduce him to my parents."

"Of course you can." I was pleased for Rueben, as he had been longing for this day to come, to be with his dad.
I also believed it would be good for him. He had witnessed so much in the past with Terence and me; I decided it would be good for his self-esteem, to meet the other side of his family. The family that he had never known.

Oliver and Rueben set off later that night. As I waved Rueben good bye, his eyes spoke to me. I could see for the first time that my baby felt lost. I was not mature enough to understand why, and could not comprehend it. Although as a child I suffered, I did not think about the feelings of my own children. I did not think whatever I went through, would cause them to suffer.

The next day, I headed to Sandra's taking Keisha and Shekira with me. I missed Rueben. I was not used to any of my children going away. I needed the time to pass quickly.

At Sandra's, everyone was nice to me and made me feel special.

"What's that?" I asked. Watching the bits floating on top of the water in a pot on Sandra's stove.

"Mushroom tea," Dee piped up merrily.

"Mushroom tea! I've never heard of that before."

"They're magic mushrooms. Have some; they'll make you feel happy," Sandra suggested pouring out some of the tea into a large cup.

The tea was green grey in colour and smelt like wet washing that had been left for days without being dried.

"Drink it down in one go," Dee advised.

Everyone was laughing. 'These mushrooms, must be good'! I gulped the tea down as fast as possible. I wanted to be laughing too.

"Yuck! It's disgusting."

"How do you feel?" asked Sandra.

"Fine, but it tastes really horrible."

They all laughed even more at my screwed up face; they thought my behaviour was hilarious.

"I feel sick." The tea had made me nauseous.

"It's okay the feeling will pass," Marie advised rubbing my back to relieve my discomfort.

She was right. About twenty minutes later sitting on a tall stool in Sandra's kitchen, with the feeling of sickness gone, my mind began to play tricks.

"The front door looks weird."

"What do you mean?" Sandra asked.

"It looks wobbly," I confided.

"Try and walk," Dee suggested.

Standing up, I began to shake. Taking each step slowly, my legs felt like were going to give way. Everyone fell into fits of giggles. I wanted them to help me, but I had become the joker of the pack.

After laying down waiting for the dizziness to wear off, I headed home, promising myself I would never take anything like that again. I always seemed to promise my self this but always got into something else. At home, I sorted out myself and prepared for Rueben's arrival the next day.

When Rueben arrived, he appeared lively, rather than subdued. This pleased me. Oliver said he had introduced him to his mum and dad, and some of his cousins. They all spoiled him by giving him money and clothes and most of all love.

"Did you have a nice weekend?" Oliver asked me.

"Yes thanks it was great!" No way was I going to confess what had happened.

"I'll contact you to take Rueben on a regular basis."

'Brilliant,' I thought. At last Rueben would have two parents and not one. Unfortunately Oliver did not keep his promise, and it was not long until Rueben was subdued again. Though he knew I loved him, being a boy, he needed his father's love!

My new friendships soon turned my life around for the worst. By Christmas mum and dad stopped visiting on a regular basis. They could see the negative changes in my life. There appeared to be no room for them. I started to feel lost. I was not used to this. I would always see mum or speak to her at least once a day. We had a tight bond.

"Fiona, you're so nice," my new friends would say, giving me a false sense of security.

"You're really pretty." This was one of Dee's favourite catch-phrases.

It was not long before I felt used.

"Can you do me a favour?" Sandra asked one day. "We're going to London for the weekend, me, Dee, Susie and Marie, I need you to baby-sit?"

Keeping my anger to myself, I still did not know how to speak up. I could not dispute the unfairness of the situation. 'Why had they not asked me to come?' I could hear the words screaming in my head.

"Of course I will." Like a fool, I agreed, reluctantly. "Go and have a good time," I encouraged them.

I sat and watched whilst everyone packed their bags and set off to London to have a good time, without me. From

Friday night to Saturday evening, I babysat Sandra's five children along with my three. Stunned by what was happening I began to reflect. Here I was five months from parting with Terence, taking ecstasy, in love with a man who did not care for me, friends who were doing what they wanted with me, and hardly any contact with my family.

So much had happened in such a short space of time. History had come into the present time. I was under Sandra's power again. Doing as I was told, from making the coffees, to cleaning up after everyone. The only difference with this situation was that Sandra needed my help and I needed hers, so I succumbed. She was deeply depressed because of her problems with Martin, and was in no fit state to stand on her own two feet. I became her crutch, and because of Nigel and the relationship she had with him, she became mine.

Late one evening, the week before Christmas, I was staying at Sandra's house with the children when there was a knock on the door. I had gone to bed leaving Sandra downstairs. I could hear Sandra calling.

"Who is it?"

"It's me," I could hear a man's voice. A voice, which I recognised.

"Fiona," Sandra called up to me. "Oliver's here to see you."

Oliver! What did he want at this time of the evening.'

"Hello, what's happened?" I asked Oliver, hanging over the banister.

"Nothing, I thought I'd come and visit you."

"Oh," I was surprised that Oliver wanted to see me and had come to find me at Sandra's house.

"I'll leave you two to talk," suggested Sandra, exiting through the sitting room door.

I sat silently whilst Oliver smiled raising his eyebrows, confident about his visit.

"What time are you going home?" Oliver was now looking at me with lustful eyes.

"Going home?"

"Yes," Oliver replied.

"I'm not going home. It's late and I've planned to stay the night here," I told him.

"Well, why don't you leave the children here, and let me and you go back to your place," suggested Oliver.

"What about Rueben, haven't you come to see him?"

"Yes, but it's late, I'll see him tomorrow."

I did not believe him. He was making suggestions. He was expecting me to go home with him. I had my morals and I was going to stick to them.

"I'm staying here."

"I'm too tired to drive back to London, ask Sandra if I can sleep on her settee." Oliver was determined he was going to spend the night with me.

Since Oliver had travelled from London to Cambridge, Sandra and I agreed it would be wise for him to stay in case he fell asleep whilst driving. We did not want the responsibility of an accident, so Sandra allowed him to sleep on her settee.

"Here's a blanket."
Spreading the blanket over himself on the settee, Oliver made himself at home.

"Come and lay down with me," Oliver beckoned patting a space next to him that he had made for me. He was smiling again, raising his eyebrows. 'I can have you anytime I want,' he had once remarked in the past. Infuriated by this memory, I rejected his advances.

"I'm going to bed, goodnight."
Oliver's face dropped. His smile disappeared. I had my revenge, but wondered why everyone seemed to think they had the permission to do what they wanted with me.

Later, at around two o'clock in the morning there was a big bang on Sandra's back window. It was Nigel wanting to talk to me. Lucky me, I had two men chasing after me! But it was Nigel I wanted.

"I've got a drug problem," Nigel explained, after Oliver had left in a huff. "I've been taking cocaine, and I don't ever want to take drugs again. I love you. I want to be with you for the rest of my life. Will you have me back?"
How could I resist. I had been longing for him to come back for the past six months and it was now happening. I did not understand about his drug problem. I did not know you could get addicted to this kind of thing. I just thought you took some when you wanted to have a good time. All I wanted at this moment was to have him back.

As Nigel lent forward to kiss me, a little pipe fell from under his sleeve.

"Whoops!" Picking it up quickly, Nigel pleaded, "I promise I won't do it again, I'll stay with you twenty-four seven. I won't go out."

I wondered what he was going on about. It was only a pipe!

CHAPTER 10

A YOUNG MAN'S SLAVE

Getting back with Nigel made me feel like I had something that every woman wanted. Not only did Samantha try to get him back, with no success, there were a lot of other women who wanted to be with him. I was hardly surprised. Because Nigel was a drug dealer, he was very popular. The women loved his charming ways. But he loved me and I loved him.

Nigel kept his promise. He stayed in, only going out to get some weed whenever necessary. He was a brilliant dad towards my children. He would make Shekira's bottles, feed her and change her nappies. His patience and caring towards them made me love him more. As we became closer Nigel began to confess.

"Me and Martin made thousands of pounds in the summer selling drugs."

"What did you do with it?" I did not understand the illegality of what they had been doing.

"We blew it on partying and taking drugs. But now I'll get a job and look after you." Nigel concluded. But he never did.

Within weeks, Nigel took away my fears about white people, due to his main circle of friends being white. Because he was adopted by white people his upbringing and outlook on the English culture was different from mine. Although this was the case, Nigel still suffered some racism. Not just from white people but also from black people. Black people would exclude him because of the way he spoke and because his cultural mannerisms were different in the way he expressed himself. I would feel sorry for him. He longed to be included by them, whereas I wanted to be included by the white people. And at this stage of my life it was more difficult for me to mix as I had previously only mixed with blacks. Regardless my reggae music and the way I dressed slowly disappeared from my life; to be replaced by house music and drugs in a white orientated atmosphere.

It was not long before I found out I was pregnant.

"I can't keep it," I told Nigel. "I'll never be able to cope or afford another child."

"I love you, whatever you decide I'll stand by you," he promised.

"It doesn't cost much to look after a baby," Sandra claimed after I confided my fears to her. "Milks free because you can breast feed and you can buy Terry nappies which you can wash and re-use," she insisted.

Thinking through her words, Sandra was right. The only thing I would have to worry about would be clothes. Once Nigel had a job everything would be alright.

Everything was fine for a while until Nigel started to stay away from home on the occasional nights.

"I was out with my mates," he would say. I would always believe him. I had no reason not to. Nigel was young. He enjoyed the company of his friends.

It was not until I repeatedly had dreams about Nigel seeing Dee, that I became disturbed. Not understanding why, but I felt the dream did not mean what I was seeing. It meant Nigel was seeing someone of that name, and not the Dee that I knew.

I tried to put the re-occurring dreams down to my disappointment with myself, for becoming pregnant again, and my fears of Nigel leaving me. Since leaving school my life consisted of having babies and broken relationships. With hardly any money, the outlook on my future was bleak.

The pregnancy had some benefits for me; it stopped me from having to join in taking drugs, giving me a focus away from the life I was heading into. The only thing I would do, was smoke weed which I enjoyed. It was like a sedative for me. I still felt lonely and trapped, so smoking was my only comfort.

Nigel soon began to stay out all weekend rather than the occasional nights. Because of my dream, my suspicions were aroused.

"I'm off now," Nigel stated as usual one day. It was mid afternoon, on Friday, the time he would always leave.

"What time will you be back?"

"In time for dinner," he promised.

Even though Nigel did not provide for me, I provided for him from my welfare benefits, believing he would soon get a job.

"Let's have a quiet evening in tonight," I suggested. "Watch a video and relax together, we haven't done that in a long time." I wanted Nigel for myself. For one weekend at least.

"That sounds good to me," he agreed.

After seeing Nigel off, I rushed back into house preparing a list in my mind of the things that I was going to do, to ensure a good evening. 'Clean the house from top to bottom, play with the children, in fact I'm going to clear out my drawers and airing cupboard,' I thought. It was one of those jobs that had got left behind. 'This will help me past my time away.'

Whilst cleaning up, in the airing cupboard, I came across two very small pipes. The pipes were small and were made out of metal. I remembered they were the same as the one that had fallen out of Nigel's sleeve on the night he had asked me to go back with him. I had chosen to ignore it, as I did not understand. But now there were two. Putting the pipes to one side, I decided to ask Nigel what they were for when he arrived home.

My mission to clean, led me to find things that I did not know were hidden in my house. In my bedroom draw, I found some test-tubes. 'How strange'. I could not work out what they were for.

When he arrived, I approached him anxious for a reply.

"I've found some metal pipes and test-tubes. What are they for?"

Nigel did not respond. His smiling face had now become serious; I had not seen him like this before.

"What are they for?" I questioned again expecting an answer.

"What have you done with them?" Nigel asked heading upstairs.

"They're on the top of the dresser."

Running ahead of Nigel, passing him on the landing to show him where they were, shock and anger took over.

"I don't believe it!" I screamed.

Shekira had a partly cracked test-tube in her hand. I had not noticed her going up the stairs and entering the bedroom.

"That's it; they're going in the bin."

Picking up the rest of the test-tubes and the pipes, I ran down the stairs to put them in the bin. Nigel running behind me, tripped up. So I quickly hid them in the kitchen whilst I went to see if he was okay.

"Where are they?" Nigel shouted as he ran back into the bedroom. His eyes had widened. He had beads of sweat rolling off his forehead and was now frothing from the mouth with rage.

"I'm not telling you until you tell me what they are for and why you need them, you're not a scientist so they must be for something," I insisted.

Snap, snap. Nigel switched. Grinning, uncannily he began to break apart my chest of drawers.

"Tell me where they are," he demanded.

"They're……" The ringing sound of his mobile phone interrupted my speech. Looking at me fiercely Nigel picked it up silently, before he answered. It was one of his friends asking him if he was ready to go out. Nigel had no plans to stay in with me as arranged, so when he came off the phone I faced him again.

"What's going on?" I confronted slipping on the rug in the bedroom. To stop myself from falling, I tried to grab hold of Nigel.

"Help!" I pleaded falling backwards onto the bed. I was worried about hurting my unborn baby.

Unexpectedly, Nigel struck me across the face, just like Terence had, for the first time whilst I was pregnant. Devastated and shocked, I made my way through the front door and into the cold dark night dressed in a short skirt, sandals and my hair uncombed; furious at what had just happened. I did not know where to put my feelings. Marching through the streets crying with despair, people were looking at me as though I was peculiar. I did not know where I was going or what to do. Another blow added to my experiences. Walking and walking and walking, with nowhere to go and nowhere to hide. I wanted mum. I needed to see her warm and gentle smile. I needed her to hold me. To tell me that everything was going to be alright. However, I could not go there. Mum did not want anything to do with my new life. She was disappointed that I was with Nigel. Looking after him, feeding him, and caring for him, whilst he treated me like a doormat.

"You know what to do if someone's not treating you right," she once said when I had told her about Nigel's behaviour. "Don't complain," she had continued.

Mum was right, but with my emotional attachment, I could not leave him. He was my master, and I was his slave.

I soon found myself at Sandra's house. I needed to calm down. To collect my thoughts.

Soothing my pain, Sandra rocked me to and fro, in her arms, as my tears flooded out.

"Oh dear, don't cry, everything's going to be alright. He's probably having a come down," she explained.

"A come down? What's a come down?"

"When someone's taken cocaine, it takes three days to come out of their system. Then they get angry and agitated."

"Why's that?"

"Because they go on such a high. When reality stares them in the face, they can't handle it." Sandra explained confidently like a tutor educating her student. Her explanation made sense. I began to remember those times when Nigel would be overly happy then suddenly change within two days. He would sometimes be moody and would say he was depressed for no apparent reason.

After calming down, I made my way home with Sandra by my side. I wanted to make things right with Nigel. It was not his fault, he had a problem and I wanted to help. I justified his action, because of my feelings for him.

"I'm sorry, really really sorry." Nigel was crying.

"It's okay, I understand." I reassured him.

"I can't go out with you any more, I can't believe that I hurt you." Nigel's honesty, to me was commendable.

"Let's forget it happened and move on," I insisted.

"I love you," Nigel whispered in my ear, cuddling me as always with his big strong arms. Overlooking the whole incident still not knowing what the test-tubes or the pipes were for, Nigel and I carried on as though this incident had not happened.

The rest of my pregnancy was spent in poverty. I had one pair of shoes, which was a broken down pair of sandals. I had no maternity wear, as I just could not afford it. Nigel clearly had no intention of working or providing for me and his unborn baby. What welfare benefits I had, were used not only to meet his needs, but also for the coming birth of our baby. I also did all the cooking and cleaning whilst Nigel sat back in front of the TV, smoking weed, watching us, like a lion guarding his prey. My mum used to say; "it's better to be at the mercy of God than at the mercy of man." This was definitely true in the case of Nigel and I. Because Nigel was a charmer I was at his mercy like everyone else he had gone out with. It was the same thing with his mum; he knew how to manipulate a situation to get his own way with her. All women appeared to like him.

In the month of August, I gave birth to my fourth child, another daughter, Tonika. Nigel and Natasha were there. Regardless of my situation, to bring new life into the world was always a blessing for me. At visiting time I met Nigel's parents for the first time. They were very nice and accepted me and my other children. Nigel was overjoyed with the birth of his daughter. For about two weeks, he began to pull his weight around the house. He washed up, he cooked and he cleaned. I felt there was hope after all until he had a surprise for me.

"I need to tell you something," Nigel confessed as we cuddled up in bed for a quiet night.

"Go on then, what is it?" I enquired happily.

"I want to find my birth parents, especially my mum, just to know what she looks like," he claimed.

"That's okay; do you want me to help you?"

"No, I'm going to America, I don't know how long for, but I have to go."

Numbed by what Nigel was telling me, I headed to the bathroom to take things in. Whilst thinking things through, I realised I had an opportunity to break free from Nigel. Although he had begun to help me domestically, it did not seem worth the hassle of having him with me. My house had become run down, but restorable. Suddenly a feeling of freedom overwhelmed me. Nigel going away meant I could pick up the pieces of my life whilst I had not fallen in too deeply.

"Alright, you go, I wish you the best of luck," I finally responded, giving Nigel my full blessing.

Once Nigel departed for America, mum, dad and Mirianne arrived unexpectedly, armed with paint and paint brushes.

"We've come to revitalize your house," Mirianne confided. "Now he's gone don't take him back," Mum advised.

This pleased me. My relationship with my family could now be restored along with my household. My family had drawn away from me because they could not bear to see me go down hill in life. Nigel's presence demanded a lot of my time and attention, causing me to neglect those who were important to me. Sadly, three weeks after his departure, a message arrived. Nigel was coming home. I was still vulnerable to his whims, therefore taking him back was normal. This did not go down too well with my parents. I had let them down. Again!

In America Nigel did not find his parents and would use the fact that he was adopted against me as an excuse for his bad behaviour. Whenever we had a dispute, or whenever he wanted to do what he wanted, Nigel would say, 'I don't know who I am. I'm adopted.'

My dreams about Dee were now becoming more vivid. My instincts were also speaking to me. This dream was going to come to pass. Nigel was up to something, and I was ready to find out what it was. He was still sleeping out. Partying and leaving us with no money. Although he had some money, I suspected from drug dealing.

"He's seeing a girl called Dee; she likes her E's (ecstasy)," Susie confessed. She had turned up unexpectedly with Sandra first thing in the morning.

Sitting looking at me blankly they waited for my, response.

"How do you know?" I eventually asked.

Curiosity set in. Although I did not trust Susie because of a remark she had made in the past. 'I don't like black women but I like black men,' she had said. I found myself willing to hear what she had to say because of my dream.

"He's been boasting about it, we've just been to one of his friends, who said he didn't think it was right, you're pregnant and there's Nigel being deceitful behind your back. I've seen him with her," she claimed.

"When?"

"To be honest I've dropped him off at hers before and now I feel guilty," confessed Susie. "He goes out raving a lot with her. He's always out with her."

"How long has he been seeing her?"

"Quite a while," she said.

I felt the anger rage up inside of me. Not only had he cheated on me, but everyone else knew about it.

"What colour is she?" I asked

"White, but please don't tell him I told you," she pleaded.

I did not want to agree, but did. Susie had been involved in the problems in my life, but now she wanted to be honest.

"She's also got relatives in America. I think that's where Nigel stayed when he went there."

The information was too much to cope with. The pain in my heart became stronger as the realisation of the depth of his deceit became known.

"Seriously, she goes there sometimes herself," Susie continued.

Everything made sense, the one way ticket, the nights out, money issues and the silly excuses. One excuse was he had been locked up over night for stealing a bike. I did not know much about the police system so I believed what he had said.

"Thanks for telling me, I'll deal with this when he gets home." Ironically, he had not come home yet from the night before. This time I had some ammunition.

It was early afternoon that day when Nigel strolled in. He had a smug look on his face, a look that I had not noticed before. As he opened his mouth to say the usual, 'I'm sorry,' I told him not to speak another word and confronted him with the situation. This time I was not going to keep quiet.

"Where have you been?" I asked the usual question and he gave the usual answer.

"I was out with the boys raving and we've just got back."

"You liar," I shouted.

"You're mad," he shouted back.

"No I'm not; you've been seeing someone else. Her name's Dee."

Nigel's expressions gave the answer. He had failed to keep his promises. I found out that Dee was a well educated woman from a wealthy background. She was at university in London studying law to become a barrister. When Nigel admitted he was having an affair with her, he also admitted that he had liked her from school, stabbing deeper into the wound that was already in my heart.

"I'm sorry; I think I have a problem with black women. I don't trust them, I think it's because my mum adopted me. I feel rejected. I can't cope without you," Nigel explained crying.

Because Nigel showed remorse and I loved him, I took him back, and again as usual, he stayed in only going out to get weed. This lasted for a few days until he had gained his confidence, back in me again.

I soon realised that Nigel had a thing about white women. He was always lavishing the attention they gave him. His previous excuse of not trusting black women somehow appeared true. I was not sure if it was because of his upbringing or if it was a passion of his. In fact, most of the black men in that circle and lifestyle had white women, and some of the black women had white boyfriends. It seemed to me, like a fashion thing. Leaving no place for black women, unless they were willing to have a white boyfriend. Admittedly, I was not because of my cultural differences. Nigel soon began to sleep around with them, making me feel worthless. It was as though he was paid for his time. Although I had no proof, I would hear rumours about the women who would buy him clothes, drugs and pay for him to go out. Sexually they would do the things that I would not do. It was as if he was a male prostitute.

Nigel's mental abuse began to wear me down. I needed to know the truth. I would ask him about the rumours. He would say they were not true, and I would always believe him as I was afraid to believe what everyone was saying, through fear of having a breakdown. My mind had become weak. But soon I'd had enough. Something inside me snapped, and I begun to stick up for myself.

"You make me sick, I know you're seeing someone else," I screamed at Nigel.

"You bitch!" Nigel shouted back, suddenly heading for my throat.

With his hands wrapped tightly around my neck, Nigel began to shake me. I became scared for my life. The man I loved was trying to kill me. He was like a monster. His eyes protruding out of their sockets, his lips clenched tightly, with foam at the corner of his mouth. Nigel kicked and punched me to the floor, as though he was beating on a piece of meat. I could feel each blow of the connecting punches all over my body. Confused, I believed Nigel loved me, to have behaved in this matter. I justified this, as Terence was the same. He loved me, and would beat me up, because of the way he had felt about me.

After this incident, I became seriously ill. I could not eat, drink or swallow. Nigel did not care; he would not help me around the house or with the children so Rueben became the crutch of my life. I would send him to school on the bus. He would take Keisha who was four and a half years old with him, and drop her off to nursery on the way and then he would go off to school by himself. Rueben was only eight at the time. He even cooked dinner under the instructions that I gave him as I was bed bound. I had lost all sense of reality. Nobody wanted to help. They had given up on me. Two weeks later, I was diagnosed with glandular fever and was admitted to hospital for a week due to dehydration. But this did not stop Nigel from beating on me. When I came out of hospital he strangled me and kicked me in front of one of his female friends. The strangling and the beatings became a part of our relationship. I lost who I was and my life now consisted of pleasing Nigel. I was desperate. I just wanted him, to make me a part of his life.

CHAPTER 11

DIRECTED BY DREAMS

Just before the beginning of the school summer holidays, my little sister arrived unexpectedly, insisting that I enrolled for an 'Access Course,' which she had done the previous year. She saw my potential and wanted the best for me.

"You can start in September if you enroll now," my sister had said.

The course was equivalent to 'A' level standard and would give me a new start on the road of education.

"Come on Fiona, think about it. A new life! Don't let him bring you down, do something whilst you can," she further encouraged.

Mirianne was right. I was now twenty six years old with four children and an unhopeful future. What did I have to lose? A neighbour had once informed me, 'when the children get to a certain age you don't get welfare benefits for them.' She said. 'If you did not have any experience or education it would be hard to find a job, plus at my age its even harder, nowhere wants you.' She continued and said, 'I now have to live with my daughter because I can't make ends meet. Try and do something now,' she advised.

Remembering her words, and reflecting on what Mirianne was saying, I agreed. 'I might as well do something constructive in my trapped situation'. With my emotions heightened as Nigel was still beating me up and I was finding it hard to leave him, it felt right to do something positive. If we should ever split up at least I would come out with something that I had achieved within the darkness of my life.

My decision to study had a big impact on Nigel and our relationship as he decided to study law. My influence had rubbed off on him. So he went on an enrolment test to do an access course in London. Nigel qualified, so this meant him living there. This was a positive move as far as I was concerned. I would have the space to study, get my life back as well as setting up a good routine set for myself and the children.

Throughout the summer holidays we prepared for the beginning of our courses. Our relationship appeared to have a bright future, with both of us doing something positive. For once during our relationship, I could see the sun shining until I had another dream just before Nigel left for London.

"I've just dreamt a young man walking through the front door with a suitcase in his hand; he was black and looked like a well known champion boxer," I told Nigel as we woke up one morning.

"You're going to see someone else behind my back," Nigel claimed half jokingly.

"Never, you know I'm not like that," I responded laughing back.

It felt good to see Nigel worried, for once, about what I might do rather than my worries about him. Wrestling with my mind, to understand the dream, I knew I would not go off with someone else. I loved Nigel regardless of everything, and had no intentions of being with anybody else.

September arrived, and I enrolled for college. Touring around the college, I spotted a small room which had advertising cards pinned on the wall. It was the accommodation office. What a good idea, I thought. I could rent a room in my house, and earn some extra money. Also I was used to having another adult in the house and could do with the company. As I entered the accommodation room, I saw a young black lady, and black man looking through the accommodation book. The young guy looked worried.

"Hello," I greeted them. "Are you looking for a room?"

"Yes," they replied.

"Is it for both of you?"

"I've got a room," answered the young lady. "But he hasn't," she continued pointing at the young man.

"Where are you from?" I enquired.

"London. If he doesn't find a room soon, he cannot start his course," the girl spoke for the man.

"I'll rent you a room," I told him.

Although I would have preferred to have a female lodger, because of the children, I felt sorry for this man and wanted to help him. I also was sure Nigel would not mind.

"Thanks." The young man was very grateful.

"What's your name?"

"Richard."

"I'm Fiona, what are you studying?"

"I'm doing an economics degree."

"Okay, you can move in straight away if you want."

We arranged for him to come round that day to see the room. Richard liked it very much, and we agreed on a price, and a moving in date. It was when he arrived at my house and came through the front door with his suitcase I realised, he was the man from my dream. He was the same build and darkness as the boxer in my dream and had the same looks. The scenario was exactly how it was in my dream. The dream had come to pass.

Richard was a very nice man. He was an African who had tribal marks on his face. He explained that this was a traditional thing to have done. After long conversation, he asked the inevitable.

"Do you have a boyfriend?"

"Yes, you will see him at weekends as he is studying in London," I told him.

Richard showed me the utmost respect. He was never rude or insinuated anything sexual to me. We became good friends.

Telling Nigel about my new lodger was difficult. He said he did not mind. He insisted that he trusted me. On meeting Richard, Nigel could tell Richard was not a threat to our relationship. In fact, they got on very well. Richard kept himself to himself whenever necessary and joined in with us at the appropriate times. Having Richard around made me feel safe. Nigel would control himself, to show Richard he was a nice person. However, this was not lasting.

By the end of the first term, his old habits crept back. He would insult me by calling me names, because I was getting on well with my studies, and he was having difficulties with his. I would feel embarrassed in front of Richard. He would look at me with great sadness.

To pacify Nigel and to keep the peace, I helped him out by letting him copy one of my essays, which was relevant to what he was doing. He needed to produce an essay as part of the assessment for the next stage of his course. He got 'A' plus for it, a better mark than I did. I just did not want Richard to see the violent side of him.

Soon Nigel stayed mainly in Cambridge. He appeared to have the drug problem again. I assumed he was addicted to cocaine because of what Sandra had told me. In London he had been mixing with major drug dealers who he had met there.

"Where are you going?" I would ask.

"None of your business," he would sneer.

If I insisted on an answer, Nigel would always strangle me. He would insist on making things better by sleeping with me, even if I did not want to.

Nigel just could not change. He was always going in and out of the house, sleeping out whenever he wanted. As my mum's words ran through my head, 'it is better to be an old man's darling than a young man's slave,' I began to reflect on my situation. Nigel was younger than me and I had become his slave financially, physically, sexually and mentally. He never spent money on food, yet he would eat everything as soon as it was brought, leaving me with no choice to borrow food and money from the neighbours. I was always having to scrimp and scrape to feed the children. Nigel was bully

Mentally I was scarred; along with running the household and taking his abuse, I had to think for him, finding solutions for his problems. He would constantly be in debt to drug dealers, and they would always be after him for money. There was a time when me and the children had to leave home, because one of the drug dealers had threatened to kidnap us, to get at Nigel. We stayed for a week in Janet's back room on a mattress on the floor. It was horrendous.

Suppressed by my emotions; I surrendered to Nigel's whims. The last straw came when I had a dream about a slim white woman sitting on a chair, legs crossed, in a lady-like fashion, looking at me. Her hair was tied up in a bun. She wore bright red lipstick, and she was pregnant! On waking I knew in my heart Nigel was going to get someone pregnant, and this was the woman. Destiny could not be changed. Why me? I confronted Nigel about the dream. I told him what I believed, our fate would be.

"You're crazy!" he had said. But my woman's instinct would not allow me to let this dream pass from my mind.

In the May of my first year, I threw Nigel out. My exams were due, and I refused to let Nigel spoil this important time for me. He continued his habit of strangling me whenever he felt like it, and calling me names, as he pleased. I could not take any more disruptions or any more pain. Studying was my chance to better myself to improve my life. Not just for me, but also for my children. They were always quiet, especially Rueben, because of the environment they were in.

On one occasion, mum had turned up unexpectedly. Although my family hardly visited anymore, they were still concerned for the welfare of the children.

"Rueben's distressed. He's scared. He believes Nigel is going to kill you. You'll have to leave him," she had said.

"No he's not; you don't want me to be with him," I accused.

Because mum and dad did not visit me as much anymore, I had refused to accept their comments. Their comments made me rebel. I was determined that things were going to work out with me and Nigel, in front of everyone. But deep down, I had resigned myself to the truth. Nigel was not going to change.

The end of the college year arrived, and I took my exams. I passed my 'Access Course' with flying colours, qualifying for a place to study for a degree in Social Policy, Health and Welfare, to start in September that year.

Richard left for London to stay with his family for a while. He said he would not be renting at mine anymore. He said, now that he was familiar with Cambridge he would rent accommodation with some other students on his course. I believed, Nigel had scared him away.

During that summer, Nigel would not leave me alone. He kept coming round begging me to take him back, but I refused. Although I was in immense pain and distress, I knew I could not turn back. My heart was talking to me. Nigel was having a relationship with someone else, but he refused to admit it.

"You want your cake and eat it, don't you," I would accuse. But he would always deny it.

Nigel was on a high, supremely confident. His new friends from London had changed him into more of a monster than before. He became spiteful. One night he arrived, forced me to sleep with him, ordered a pizza for himself, and left. I meant nothing to him. My life consisted of abuse, and there was no one to turn to for help.

I soon had another dream. I was looking through a window of a house around the corner where Natasha lived. I could see a blonde woman with her hair roughed up in a bun holding a mixed-raced baby. This confirmed, to me, that my previous dream of a girl being pregnant was going to come true. It was painful not having any proof. All I could do was wait.

That summer Nigel made my life hell along with the so-called friends I had made, they all carried on as though he was something special, entertaining him and hiding what he was doing. Making a mockery of me.

"I have a soft spot for Nigel," Dee teased one day, knowing that I was traumatised over his behaviour.

Her remark, reminded me of when I was with Oliver, and how desolate everyone had made me feel; now they were all doing it again. I had to take the pain slowly and quietly, pretending that I did not know they were laughing at me. I even helped Dee to paint her bedroom in a desperate ploy to find the truth. She still would not give me any information about Nigel. The only person in the group who stood by me in this situation was Sandra. She said if she had to, she would give up their friendship for me. To me, this showed the depth of her love for me. So I put more of my trust in her.

Meanwhile, trauma took over my life and devastation set in; I couldn't take the hurt anymore. I couldn't hold it in. Within weeks I went down to seven and a half stone in weight. I wanted to die. My life was not worth living. I did not want to exist anymore. No one appeared to care for me, not even my family. As I downed the bottle of tablets, I soon felt better. The decision to end my life was worth it. No more hurt and no more pain. I would be doing everyone a big favour. Including the children. As I laid my head on the pillow that night, for once in my life I felt truly secure. I was going to a place where nothing or no one could hurt me ever again. I planned for Natasha to stay the night so that the children would not be left alone in the morning. Natasha was always there in the shadows of my life, but I felt like I did not know her any more because of our different lifestyles. I had changed. Admittedly I had, on the quiet, been taking speed, which one of my neighbours had introduced to me. It was a drug which would keep you awake. It helped me in my times of study along with smoking weed. The speed would help numb some of the pain but the side effects would cause depression.

Waking up the next morning after taking the bottle of tablets, I was upset for being alive. I looked at the children as they, one by one, came into my bedroom.

"Morning mum," they spoke one by one.

Changing my mind, my children were something worth living for. They needed me. I knew I had to pull myself together for their sake. Besides, God was not ready for me to die. Reality stared me in the face. I did have hope of a good future. I was due to start my degree course. I reminded myself, the degree course would give me an education and help me to do something constructive later on. I told Natasha what I had done the night before, and she informed the rest of the family. They gathered around me and were very upset to begin with. They told me to be strong, and then I never saw them again for about another six months. Only Natasha. They did not believe I was going to change my life. I had made so many promises, and never kept them.

After I had started my degree, Nigel decided to confess.

"You're right. I've got someone pregnant. Because of your dream I was too scared to tell you. I love you and want to be with you for the rest of my life. It's finished with me and her," he declared.

"You're having a laugh... it's too late." Nigel repulsed me. The long nights, the anxiety, the not knowing, the humiliation, and most of all the cruelty, (physical and sexual). For the first time in weeks, I could relax. My dreams had come true. I knew my instincts were right and I was not mad. All I needed was a confession from Nigel, and now I had one.

"Does she live on the next street up from Natasha?" I asked confidently.

"No, why do you say that," Nigel lied.

"Just wondered," I replied.

Nigel suddenly said he had to go.

"I'll be back." He was smiling and confident that his confession would mean everything between us was now alright. But he was mistaken! Shortly after him leaving, Natasha arrived.

"I know where the girl lives." Natasha insisted.

"What girl?"

"The girl you believed Nigel's been seeing, you were right, she lives around the corner from me."

Natasha had known about my dreams and so did everyone else. Persuading them that I knew it was real had been a big problem. I was told on many occasions that it was all in my mind.

Because Nigel had just left, I believed that he had gone there, so me and Natasha agreed that she would drop me off and wait for me at her house. She did not want to get involved through fear of any reprisals. We decided I would knock the door of the house where Nigel parked his car. If I did not see his car then I would have to go back to Natasha's and wait.

On arriving at the street, Nigel was standing in a garden with a lady who appeared slightly older. Her hair was roughed up in a bun. She looked exactly how she did in my dream. And she was pregnant!

"What are you doing here?" he asked softly, choking back his words.

"I thought you said you'd finished with her. You're nothing but a lying cheat. Now get lost and stay out of my life."

The woman, (Caroline), looked at me smirking as though she had something that I wanted.

"And you," I declared pointing my finger in her face. "You can have him."

The mental fight was now over. I was free from the emotional turmoil of not knowing where I stood with Nigel. Although I was not with him, the torture he put me through was enough to push me over the edge. But I praise God for forewarning me. He was on my side.

Shortly after I arrived home, Nigel turned up with all his things.

"I've moved my things out of her house." He claimed. "I'm moving in with you."

"No you're not! I don't want anything to do with you again."

"I'm not going anywhere," he threatened, forcing his way into my bedroom to pack his things away.

I tried my hardest to get rid of him but he just would not leave. I soon became distraught. I did not want to be with him but was scared of what he would do to me. Also, for some silly reason, a part of me felt sorry for him. He would frequently cry and make false promises. Promises that he could not keep. I so wanted him to change but deep in my heart I knew he couldn't and wouldn't.

After moving back in, Nigel became violent again. One time he strangled me until I lost consciousness. When I came around, Nigel was wiping blood from my nose. To Nigel, I was better off dead than to be free without him.

In the meantime, my studies of Social Policy in relation to race and gender laid a heavy burden on my heart and I felt the need to pursue the issues. We had to answer the question, 'Is the talk of race racist within itself'. In discussion, the class was asked how they saw the black race. The responses were not what I expected. Black people were seen as violent, sexual, criminals and good only in the music field. One person related to the toy golliwog as a term for black people. I especially felt sympathy for black women in western society and their positions in relation to politics, and in the social symmetry. I could relate to them. Because of gender issues, women were treated unequally and had to fight for their rights for equality. So being a black woman meant our fight for equality was harder. This did not help my confidence in my domestic and social environment especially since the women Nigel was seeing behind my back where white, and most of the black men on the rave scene would turn their nose up at the black women, treating the white women as more superior. This sickened me and I longed to be cocooned within my black culture again.

I learned that some white people also felt inferior to black people, they did not understand the black race. They always seemed to feel intimidated by us. Studying social policy gave me a clearer view of this viewpoint. Violence by some black people, is their way of standing up for their rights, and to be heard. And many from the West Indies, turn to crime for survival. Changes in immigration laws made it impossible for them to have a work permit for a six-month stay in England. This led to a feeling of being used in the post-war era. The time when most west-Indians were invited to come over to work to build up the welfare state doing the jobs the white British did not want to do. Due to rises in unemployment after those times, immigration laws were changed. Some British people felt as though immigrants were taking over their employment opportunities. This I found insulting because most black people were employed to do menial jobs, keeping them at the bottom of the status ladder. The music industry was where a black person could be heard or seen as someone, and even in that, the image is rough and ready, a stereotyped image, which is hard to shake off.

Charmaine, a Christian black girl I knew from my course, came and stayed with me for a while. I asked her if she felt like I did, about fitting into the British society and she said no. She only really went out with white people. She said she got on better with them. Being a Christian explained her reasons. She did not see things the way the world did. She said that she perceived everyone as the same, and the type of people she mixed with, were people who were positive. It was nice having her around. She did not judge me or my poor situation. Charmaine's dad was the Pastor of a church in Luton. She had two sisters and a very caring mum. They invited us to stay with them for a weekend to get away and be spoiled. No one had ever done that for the children or me in a long time.

"Just put your feet up. We'll look after the kids," they had said.

When it was time to go home, they all prayed for me and the safety of my children. They prayed for God to come into my life and change my situation. My heart was crushed when it was time to go home, to face the reality of my dismal situation.

One morning, Nigel's violence took a turn for the worst. He had beaten me up the night before, before going off out again, and I was bruised all over. His drug problem was now out of control. His ill treatment was now unbearable. The more he took drugs the more likely it was for him to beat me up. Nigel had come home in the early hours of the morning. I believed he had been with Caroline. That morning I had got the children up to get them ready for school. After running the bath, I told them to get in it and headed for the bedroom.

"I want you to leave," I screamed taking his clothes out of the wardrobe.

Nigel shouted obscene language at me as usual and dragged me onto the bed.

"I'm not going anywhere," he screamed back, taking my clothes out of the cupboard, as if to make a statement.

He then started to smash up my bedroom with a golf club. Frightened for my life I hurried into the bathroom to check the children. For the first time in my life I thought I was going to die. Turning towards the hallway Nigel stood nervously. He had beads of sweat pouring down his face.

"I'm not leaving," he stated as he pointed the gun at me.

I knew I had to be sensible. Having a gun pointed at you by someone who was capable of pulling the trigger, was an experience that I did not think could happen to me. I rushed into the bathroom thinking I would be safe because the children were in there. But I was mistaken. Nigel pushed the door open and aimed the gun at me, in front of the children. In a frenzy, I pushed the gun away from my face and ran past him. Running through the front door to Janet's in the rain with no shoes on. Collapsing into Janet's arms, the words would not come out to tell her what had just happened. Gathering my thoughts, I remembered the children were left in the house. With Nigel!

Going home I crept into the house to meet with Nigel once again, aiming the gun at me in the presence of Rueben. Complying with Nigel was the hardest thing to do. It was the only way out of this dreadful situation.

"I need to get the children ready for school, and then we can talk," I told him gently to pacify him.

Nigel agreed, but insisted that we took the children to school together. There was no escape. Back at home, after discussing our problems, I insisted that I wanted him to leave. Nigel was not in agreement. Grabbing me by the neck, and then by my face, squeezing hard with his fingers, Nigel threw me back onto the bed. Then all of a sudden he began to cry and calmed down.

"I'm going to the shops," I told him, seizing an opportunity to leave the house but Nigel would not let me go.

The next day, when Nigel thought there was peace between us, he finally left me alone, and went out. I was now able to leave, to seek legal help from a solicitor, at the office where Natasha worked as a legal secretary. Within a few hours of telling the solicitor my story, my Affidavit was presented to the court and I was granted an emergency injunction against Nigel, with the power of arrest. This meant if he came near me or anywhere near my house, he would be arrested. This was to be activated for six months. When the warrant officer served him with the papers, he did not resist. Crying, Nigel slowly packed and left. Ashamed of what he had done.

CHAPTER 12

THE DARKNESS CONTINUES

With the court injunction in place, my life became better. I did allow Nigel to see the children at Sandra's house, but this arrangement did not last long. Nigel soon wormed his way back into my heart, and again I became emotionally attached, letting him stay with me on the odd occasion until eventually he was back in. He had been nicer to me and made up for what he had done, by cooking, cleaning and caring for the children, again!

But, as usual, this did not last long. Our relationship went further into the darkness. Caroline gave birth to a baby boy. This woman now had a part of Nigel, which to me meant, she also had a part of my life, and there was nothing I could do about it. I was now in a very vulnerable state, not just because of this situation, but also because one of my friends was murdered by her husband.

He had never been violent towards her during their marriage. But when she told him it was over, he flipped, stabbing her several times. Because of this, I needed Nigel to support me. I suppose I was desperate for his love and his attention, which he always seemed to show me, whenever there was a crisis. To me, he was the only person who really knew me, and understood my emotional needs, even though he was the cause of most of them. I was emotionally trapped.

It was at this time that I discovered that Nigel was taking not only taking cocaine, and smoking weed, but he was also taking crack. That's what the test-tubes and pipes were for.

"They mix the cocaine with baking powder, and then melt it down to purify it. Then they use a metal pipe to smoke it from. It gives them a high for a moment, then they want more to chase the feeling that they first had. They're addicted. " Sandra had confided.

Nothing was real anymore. I could not understand why anyone would want to go through all that hassle to get on a high. Besides it cost twenty pounds for one hit.

I also discovered, the drug dealers he dealt with in London, were gunmen. Once, I was in a car with Nigel, and one of these men, (who had become Susie's boyfriend), driving on the motorway when a sudden fear came over me; I sensed, this man was really evil, and felt an urgency to jump out onto the road, whilst the car was going at high speed. I resisted the temptation through fear of hurting myself. He was the same man who had hunted for me, to kidnap me because Nigel owed him money. Nigel was obviously afraid of him, as he always did as he was told. I was so scared for our lives.

Life with Nigel, became stressful again. We were still living on more or less nothing, going hungry on many occasions. I watched helplessly as Nigel dismantled the house. He was always smashing something up, if he was not beating me. Janet's prediction had come true. I was losing my possessions one by one, bit by bit.

Nigel would always smash things up whenever he was angry. Plates, cups, ornaments, until eventually I had nothing left, not even doors. The more Nigel abused me the more desperate I became, for him to love me. My emotions were in his control.

One time I was so upset with him, I knew he was still seeing Caroline, but he refused to admit it.

"I hate you," I screamed, crying. The pain of the mental torture was just too much to bear. And once again, he blew his top.

"You slut!" Foaming from the mouth, Nigel punched and kicked me to the ground, dragged me by my arm across the living room floor into the hallway, then kicked me repeatedly.

"Please, please," I begged, unable to move. But he just would not stop.

Finally, he ran into the kitchen. Lifting my head painfully off the floor, I could hardly see. Everything was a blur. Hearing the sound of cutlery, I forced my head further off the floor. Oh no! Nigel was grabbing a knife.

"Ugh!" Throwing the knife down, he ran towards me. Something was seriously wrong with me. I could feel the wetness of my blood all over my face.

"I'm sorry, I'm sorry," he repeated several times.

"I can't move," I sobbed.

My body rooted to the ground, felt as though every bone was broken. Frightened by the sight of my injuries, Nigel offered to take me to the hospital, but I refused to go. I was afraid the doctors would call social services, and have my children taken off me for being in such a bad relationship.

It was obvious to those who knew me, and to those in my neighbourhood, that Nigel was not treating me right. My appearance had gone down hill. My hair had started to fall out due to the stress, and my personality became more subdued. What communications skills I had, were now zero. I soon became immune to Nigel's violence and the mental abuse, and would walk around like a zombie. I stopped feeling any physical or mental anguish, by ignoring it. Living day to day.

There was also now the issue of my children; not only were they neglected at home, they were now becoming targets for racial abuse in the neighbourhood. They were now a little bit older, so I would let them out to play with the other kids, which created another problem. There was always some issue to make me feel hostile towards society. They were told by one girl, that black people should be slaves, and that they were the lowest in society. If there were any disputes between the children, my sister's children and mine were always blamed. If anyone picked on them, their parents would do nothing about it. One man, who was a solicitor, actually called them black bitches. On confronting him about what he said, he did not deny it, and did not apologise for his behaviour.

My immediate neighbours were not too bad towards me, and would stick by me. They were either alcoholics, drug-takers and dealers in some way, and I watched slowly a new estate of houses going downhill into a Bronx type area. A lot of the mothers and children, were in some way suffering some type of abuse from their partners or husbands. It appeared, some black people and underworld types stuck together, against those who were racist, and prejudiced towards those who were underprivileged and in abusive situations.

My college work soon suffered, leaving me with no choice but to tell my personal tutor about my home life, and the environment I was living in. One morning before college, Nigel had beaten me up whilst I was naked, in front of my children, my nephew, and the post-man. 'You whore,' he had hissed at me, throwing paint all up the walls in the hallway, then hitting me to satisfy his temper.

My personal tutor was appalled by the situation and insisted that I called him at home, at any time, day or night, and said he would pick me up if necessary. That day, social services knocked my door. Rueben had had enough too. He had broken down in the arms of his headmistress at school.

He had told her that he was worried he was going to find me dead when he got home from school. Whenever there was an argument between me and Nigel, the girls would run and cry to Rueben. He would comfort them in his room. They would huddle up together in a corner and cry, terrified, of what was going to happen. They were not fed properly and one teacher at school had told the social services that I was not caring for the children in the way that I should. Saying, that lately the children appeared scruffy, and the girl's hair was always a mess. They threatened me, and said, if I did not leave Nigel, my children would be taken into care. Feeling ashamed of myself, I tried my hardest to keep Nigel away. But it was impossible, he would always persist and wear me down.

I carried on my studies, suppressed, in a world of my own. My tutor suggested I studied domestic violence, as one of my modules to help me combat the situation, which I did. I concluded, some men were violent because they felt inadequate. They would use alcohol, and drugs to make themselves feel good about themselves, and then use that, as an excuse for their violence. It was comforting to know, that there were lots of women out there who had suffered, and were suffering, what I was going through. I realised it was not my fault, as Nigel would always tell me. He was the one with the problem.

During this time, I began to have more and more dreams. They were quite disturbing. I would dream about the next day of my life, and many things to come, and I would watch the dreams come to pass. I would always know what was going to happen next in my relationship with Nigel, which would distress me. The dreams were always to do with him, and other women. And if any one became close to me, including my neighbours, I would dream something about them to do with their lives, even the smallest of details.

Once I dreamt my neighbour sitting down with a man, who I had never seen before. He was upset about something. In the middle of them, was a cross. She said to this man, 'I am upset too, you know'. She had a ring on her finger, and showed it to me. I told her about the dream the next day, describing the man; she did not know who he was either. Because of the cross she was worried and asked me if I thought her son was going to die. Although I was worried, because of the cross, I reassured her that this was not going to happen. Some of the dreams I had, I did not know the meaning until they actually happened. Shortly after, she met a man and begun a relationship with him. They were together about two months, when she came rushing round.

"Fiona! Your dream."

"What Dream?"

"The one about the cross."

"Oh yes," I recalled.

"My boyfriend's mum has died. I just told him that I was upset too, just like in your dream. It's him you dreamt about."

Her new partner fitted the description, and he had previously given her a ring. Although she had not known him that long, she felt for him. The cross had represented his mother's death.

Nigel knew about my dreams, which was part of his frustration. He could not really hide what he was doing. He would always have to confess to me.

One time I had a dream about something one of his friends had done.

"There's a man whose been looking after his girlfriend's child, whilst she goes to work. The child has got nits, big ones which he should have noticed. Mark it down that I told you this today. I don't know who it is because I didn't see their faces," I told him the dream.

The same day Nigel came home from one of his days out.

"You're a witch," he told me.

"Why?"

"One of my friends is in trouble with his girlfriend. He looks after her son whilst she goes to work. Her son's got nits. She said he should have noticed them, because they're really big."

Once again, my dream had been confirmed.

The dreams became more frequent, and I became disturbed by them. I just wanted them to go away. An Iranian friend I had met at college, suggested I saw a spiritual counsellor who could help me.

"Write them down," the counsellor advised. "Then we could see if there is a specific pattern."

I couldn't see the relevance in what she was saying. So I never went back.

I finished the first year of my degree with a struggle. I believed that God must have been with me throughout the course. One time I had spent all night doing an essay on my computer and forgot to save it. I had switched off my computer by mistake and went off to have a bath. When I turned my computer back on, the assignment had gone. It was due in that day. After convincing my tutor that this was the case, he agreed that I could have until the next day to hand it in.

That evening, I left the children with Sandra, and headed for the college library where there was peace and quiet to re-write it. During a break, I bumped into a lady who went to church. I told her my situation, and she said she would pray for me. This gave me hope. I then wrote my essay by hand in two hours. It was better than the first one.

College was a long way from Sandra's, and I was very tired and hungry, with no money to get back. The only way out was to walk. On walking home, my feet felt as though they did not touch the ground. Taking each step, I looked at the traffic wondering if any one could see. I was being carried. Reaching Sandra's house, I could not wait to tell her what had happened.

"God carried me."

"You what?"

"God carried me!" I exclaimed with excitement. "I was tired, but I felt my feet didn't touch the ground."

This experience made me realise I was not alone. Sandra told me about a poem written by an unknown author called footprints. The person looked back on the different scenes of his life with the Lord and saw two sets of footprints. One was his and one was the Lord's. But he noticed sometimes there was only one set of footprints. This was when the man was at his lowest and saddest in life. So he turned to the Lord and said:

"In my distresses where were you?"

The Lord said, "Where there is only one set of footprints, that's when I am carrying you."

Because Sandra was a spiritual person, she understood what I meant. She would always read her bible to me, so I always felt comfortable telling her my dreams, and she would watch them with me, come to pass. Sometimes she would even interpret them for me. She would also have dreams herself, but not as often. Sometimes I would dream about something that was going to occur on our nights out, and we would watch it happen.

Sandra and I spent many a dark night together in sadness with our children wondering why bad things were always happening to us. We both had our tribulations, but no matter what, we stood by each other.

After completing the first year of my degree, although it felt good to have achieved something, I was glad to have a break from studying. So much had happened in such a short space of time. So my priority now, was to spend time with the children. To show them how much I loved them. They had suffered so much. I just wanted to make it up to them. Nigel had also finished his first year in law studies, despite his drug taking. I believed things might become better as we had both achieved something. Again, I was mistaken. Because I had an education grant, I was not entitled to full welfare benefits. The only money I could have was forty pounds a week, including child benefit. With four children and a man that would not provide, I knew I could not survive. I had no other option but to inform the social services that I could not afford to feed my children. They told me they could not help. I tried charities, to get a loan, all with no success. No government authority would help, they all turned me down. I could not go to work. I would be worse off. I would have to pay full rent, council tax, childcare, still leaving me with no money to feed the children. Telling myself, it was only seven weeks until my grant was due, I prepared myself for what was to come. I was used to going hungry occasionally, but I knew this, was going to be different.

The hunger I felt that summer was unbelievable. I had to make sure there was at least one meal a day for the children. I lived on hot drinks and cigarettes that I had scrounged from my neighbours. If I ate anything, I would feel as though I was depriving the children. Soon I started to hallucinate seeing different types of things to eat. Sometimes I'd go to eat, thinking I had something in my hand, only to find there was nothing there. It reminded me of films I had seen, where the characters are in the desert, and they see a mirage and run towards it, only to find it was an illusion.

Nigel didn't even try, to at least provide for his children. He was off doing what he wanted. He was more concerned about how he was going to feed his habit, and his relationship with other women.

At times, I would go to Natasha's and Andrea's to ask for food to feed the kids. They would go through their cupboards, and fill up bags of shopping. Even depriving their own children of some of the things they needed.

Because of the distress my hair began to fall out even more. I was so oppressed. Desperate for someone to hear me, but nobody could. I could not go to my parents and old friends for help, because of my situation with Nigel. Although mum and dad did help once. Natasha had told them how bad my situation was.

"I begrudge feeding him," mum had said. I could see her point, but wanted her to ignore her feelings and just help.

Sometimes my Iranian friend from college would bring things for the children as a treat. Iranian food that they were not keen on. But they had to eat it. It was all we had. I knew I had to hold my head up high and persevere. It was only a matter of time before this awful situation would be over.

It appeared my life was going to become more burdensome when a gypsy friend of mine popped round to see me. She was well known amongst the black community, together with her husband. They saw themselves as black, because they felt deprived by society, in the same way that the black culture was.

"Let me read your palm," she suggested.

"Alright." I would do anything for knowledge of my future.

"You're going to leave college and fall pregnant with twin boys," she claimed.

"No you're wrong. I'm finishing my course and there's no way I want more children. Not under my circumstances," I told her.

"We'll see," she said and was gone.

Autumn came, and I was out of my hunger situation. It was time for me to start the second year of my degree. I really felt like giving up, but was encouraged by one of my tutors to continue.

"How many people do you know who are in your situation. A single parent of four children, a violent partner and studying a degree full time." She had said.

She was right, I was like a single-parent, as I provided everything. And yes, I had survived my access course and the first year of my degree against all odds. Patting myself on the back, I was determined I was going to complete my course.

CHAPTER 13

MY SUPPORT

Nigel began to spend a bit more time in London with his friends. Nevertheless, when he was in Cambridge, he continued to be horrible to me. Looking towards the sky at night, I would wish upon a star. My prayer. Hoping the stars would hear me. Whenever Nigel and I had an argument and he went off, I would always wish that he would return later that night or the next day; Even though he was nasty to be, I hated being on my own, especially when it got dark. My wish for his return would sometimes come true. I did not know if it was just a coincidence, or whether someone was hearing my cries for help!

The winter months soon ended and I was in my second term. I had started on my first assignment when my mind went blank. All the information I needed to complete it was wiped out of my mind. I had studied hard that term. But nothing was registering. I had enjoyed my studies on New Left Realism, and New Right Theories on race in the social and political arenas. Now all the hard work I had put into studying this subject, had been erased from the memory bank of my mind. I tried my hardest to remember what I had learnt. Going backwards and forwards to the computer, without success, my mind was just empty. I could not go any further. I tried and tried to tap into the information in my mind, but to no avail. As the darkness overshadowed me, I had to admit, my gypsy friends words had come true. I had no choice but to give up.

"I need a break," I told my tutor.

"Yes, it's okay. You've been through a lot," he encouraged.

"You can continue your studies at anytime. Everything that you have accomplished will be credited to you when you continue," he reassured.

Nothing ever seemed to work for me. Empty and void, I sensed something else was about to happen.

"I feel sick," I said to Nigel as I awoke one morning.

"Uhm, maybe you're pregnant," Nigel responded with a big smirk on his face.

"You wish," I hissed.

Being pregnant would mean that Nigel would have even more of a hold on me. He knew things were changing between us because of my attitude towards him. I had stopped questioning him about his whereabouts. I had stopped caring about whether he was in London or in Cambridge, and I had decided I was leaving him, once and for all.

As the days progressed, the idea of being pregnant, had now become a torment in my mind.

"How could this have happened?" I questioned Nigel.

I was having contraceptive injections, so I knew I could not get pregnant, plus we were more or less having a non-sexual relationship.

"I slept with you whilst you were asleep." He laughed.

This was actually a possibility. Because of the trauma I was under, and the fact that I smoked so much weed, I would be so exhausted. I would sleep, and not hear anything what so ever. It was as though my body would shut down completely. Anyone could have done anything to me, and I would never have known. Nigel used to boast and say he would put a pillow over my face to see how long it would take me to stop breathing. When I appeared to nearly stop breathing, he would remove the pillow.

"I got scared once because you actually stopped breathing," he had told me arrogantly. Laughing as though my life did not matter.

When I saw a doctor at the surgery, and told him I was pregnant, he thought I was mad, because of the contraceptive injections I was having. He believed my home life was having an affect on my thinking, and threatened to call social services.

"You've been through a lot in your life. You are not yourself. Make sure you come back to see me in a week's time, so we can assess your situation," he told me.

The next day, enraged, I demanded to see the Manager of the doctor's surgery. She insisted I made an appointment to see a female doctor for the next day, who offered me a pregnancy test to reassure me that I was not pregnant.

"Sometimes when we have been through a lot, we believe things that aren't true." She explained. My expressions showed I was not convinced.

The pregnancy test was positive. I was pregnant! The doctors apologised and offered me their support. After having a scan, I discovered I was carrying twins. My gypsy friend was right again, but I was yet to find out whether they were boys. This was a very emotional time for me that I will never forget. Being a twin and having twins, seemed special to me.

Thinking about my four children, the tears welled up in my eyes. I could see their pitiful faces in front of me. My babies needed me and the ones inside of me needed me as well. They were all I had to show for my life. And to me that was a lot. I decided to set in my mind, a future of hard work and dedication to my children. Reassuring myself that God would not give me more than I could bear, I learnt to walk by faith and not by sight. I knew, it would be only a matter of time, before Nigel would be gone completely out of my life.

The pregnancy was very difficult. Nigel would call me names. Once, he spat in my face in front of the neighbours, and called me a whore. My mind was still set on leaving him. I was not going to let two more children witness the things that I was going through. My neighbours were very good to me and helped me with the children. I explained my situation to them, and told them of my plans to leave Nigel when the twins were born. They gave me their full support.

The twins were born, six weeks early. They were girls and not boys. They were born perfect. During my labour, Nigel shouted at me. It did not matter where we were, or what situation I was in, he was not prepared to treat me reasonably. He only bought the twins one outfit each, and that was it. It was my neigbour's that provided for them. They rallied around and provided clothes for them. The only things I needed to buy were their bottles and sanitary things.

I came out of hospital on a Friday morning, by evening Nigel was gone. He said he could not cope with everything, and left to live his own life. I had to survive all weekend with the six children on my own with no one to help. On the Sunday, I phoned mum up, hysterically, telling her, I could not cope. She came round and allowed me to sleep for most of the day. She gave me advice on how to feed the twins at the same time, which was a big help.

By the time the twins were three weeks old, Nigel had gone completely, living with his sons mum. I felt happier having the help of my neighbours with Nigel out the way. At least I could now have peace of mind.

Coping with six small children on my own was a difficult task. Sometimes Natasha would come round and help with the evening feeds, and one of my neighbours would sit with me til late at night. But, the demand on my life was too much for me to bear, so when a neighbour offered me something that she said could help, I could not resist the temptation. Anything that could take away the pain, I was willing to try.

"This will keep you awake," she advised, making a line with the white powdery substance.

"What is it?"

"It's cocaine."

I had not seen it before even though I knew, this was what Nigel and his friends took.

"Alright, what do you do?"

"You sniff it up your nose. I'll show yah," she said

I watched as my neighbour sniffed the white powder up her nose by using a rolled up bank note.

"You try it, now," she encouraged.

Which I did.

"It feels funny." I told her. I did not like the idea of sniffing something up my nose. I was worried that it would do some physical damage.

"Now take this," she said, handing me something wrapped up in cigarette paper.

"What is it?"

"Speed."

"Oh yeah, I've taken it before," I informed her.

The cocaine and the speed together worked like magic. That day, I scrubbed the house from top to bottom, cooked a nice dinner, tended to the children. We were all happy. That night, I put the children to bed with a bed time story. This was great. That night I slept the best sleep ever since coming out of hospital two weeks before. But this caused a major problem.

"Mum the twins were crying last night for their milk. I tried to wake you, but you wouldn't wake up," Keisha told me in the morning.

"You're joking. I thought they had slept through the night."

"No, they didn't. I gave them their bottles." Keisha reassured. "Good girl," I commended her, thankfully.

This soon became a habit. I would take cocaine and speed, to keep me going. At night times, Keisha would feed the twins and change their nappies. Because the cocaine and speed would wear off, I would need more to make me feel better, and to give me more energy. This was because whilst I was on it I would use up all the energy I had, burning myself out totally. It was like a vicious circle I could not get out of. I just couldn't get enough.

I deteriorated so much that, three months later, I allowed Nigel to come back. I was now like him. He was well into the party mood and so was I. I now understood the enjoyment of the drug culture. Rather than taking it to make me feel better, and to numb the pain, I would take it because I wanted to. I enjoyed it. A couple of times I joined in with Nigel, taking crack. I understood how the addiction could happen, and promised myself that I would not allow myself to go that far. After having one hit, you wanted another. The feeling of euphoria, you got, did not last long. So the desire to keep that feeling would continuously be with you. Although I stopped taking crack, I still took the other drugs. They were my support.

I soon changed from wanting to be at home looking after the children, to wanting to be away from them. My escape was to party to blank things out. I looked forward to the weekends. I was now on a cocaine binge becoming obsessed with a particular nightclub that a white guy from school was running. It made me feel good for a while. I fought my hardest to be included with all the white people there. My sister Janet worked there with another black person we knew from school. However, as black women we both found it hard to fit in. The culture was totally different. I became fascinated by the fact that I was born and bred in Britain yet did not know anything about the English culture. I so wanted to fit in. But would feel like 'a fish out of water'.

Nigel took liberties in this situation by having his friends come round until late at night, smoking weed and being off their faces, in front of the children. He also gave me heroin to smoke, which left me feeling unable to move. Thankfully, I hated it.

In the mornings, although we had both been nightclubbing and taking drugs, it would be me, that had to look after the children. The house started to become a mess, I was just about coping. The children would just humble themselves, going along with whatever was going on. I never took drugs in front of them, it was my big secret.

During this time, a white lady called Tracy befriended me. I had met her on one of my nights out. She was very

English and very ignorant about the black culture. Although she had stereotypical ideas, such as, all black men treated their women badly, which to me appeared to be true, she accepted me for who I was and my culture. Tracy never judged me, and would encourage me by saying,

"It's only for a time. You'll be able to do things like your driving, get a job, and have the things you want. You have so much potential."

Her words gave me a boost of confidence. Tracy was highlighting a life to me that I always felt I did not deserve. I wondered why she cared about me the way she did. She had her life sorted, and I was living in hell with no way out.

"You deserve the best," she claimed one time. "Choose anything you want."

Tracy bought me an expensive dress. No one had done that for me in years. She said it was her way of showing me how much she valued me. I had never bought clothes for myself, and would make do with what was given to me or buy things that were in the sale. Tracy was a great help in that area of things. She would also bring clothes, chocolate, crisps and biscuits for the children, and would take me out to lunch. She believed in me.

"I know you can't be a friend now, but I know you will be in the future," she told me. Tracy knew I was not able to give anything back to her. Either materially or personally.

I was now in one of the lowest social classes in society. With an underlying state of depression, I began to cover up by taking more drugs. Resulting in a change of my character. I became aggressive and hostile towards other people, and being black, made most of the white people I knew, scared of me. This gave me a bad name. I hated this identification.

I soon began to retaliate against Nigel. He had become abusive again, and I was not prepared to take it anymore. At times I would be violent towards him. One day I went to kill him. He had left me once too often. There was a knife on the bedroom windowsill, grabbing it, I aimed at his heart. Sitting on the bed, Nigel lifted up his leg to protect himself. The knife entered his leg instead of his heart. I needed help. I was now capable of murder.

Sometimes, I would get in such a state that I would want to hurt myself. There was a time when he would not stop calling me names. I picked up a knife and started to saw my wrist with it, right in front of him, as a cry for help. Blood started to pour out, but as usually he did not care about me, only for himself and his next fix.

"Please help me," I told the doctor. "I don't know how much more I can take."
Concerned, the doctor prescribed antidepressants.

"Take these; they will make you feel better," he promised. After getting my prescription, I took one of the tablets and threw the rest in the bin. Thinking, tablets would not resolve my problems. 'There must be more to life than hiding behind a tablet.' The doctor's suggestion, was to me, no better than taking drugs.

CHAPTER 14

A GLIMMER OF HOPE

After my visit to the doctor's, I began to question 'what was the purpose of my life,' and began to confide in Sandra, about the person I was spiritually. Even though I had always considered myself different from everyone else, I never told anyone how I felt spiritually. I told her, I was about six years old, when I was first became aware of my existence. I remember being aware that I was here on earth, on a journey, but I did not know where I was going.

"There must be another place. A place where we go, when we die," I told Sandra.

Sandra believed what I was saying; she was the first person I told about this, so I confided in her more.

"I know I came from somewhere," I continued.

"What do you mean?" Sandra asked, waiting for me to speak, with great anticipation.

"I remember looking down, seeing myself in a pram as a baby, but I don't know where I was," I told her.

Sandra explained that a friend of hers had once told her, 'where God, is he is.' This stuck in my mind. It confirmed my thoughts. I knew something was there before I was born. A different dimension. But I did not know what.

Regardless of my spiritual thoughts, I continued to go out. Having late nights, and sometimes coming home in the early hours of the morning. I continued to take cocaine and ecstasy. Consciously, I knew my life needed sorting out. But it seemed totally impossible, so I just lived for the moment.

Soon I had a new neighbour, Hayley. I had known her since we were children. Her dad and my dad had worked on the buses together, and were good friends. She had four small children, and had just come out of prison, for bottling someone in self-defense. Hayley was tall and slim. She was very kind to everyone and would give you her last. Unfortunately Hayley was mixed up. Her past nightmares had caught up with her, and she was trying to have the best in life, in the only way she knew. Hayley loved her children very much and wanted the best for them. So to get the extra things they wanted, Hayley would pay, with whatever means. One day she invited me to go along with her.

"You can have anything you want, if you come with me," she persuaded.

Thinking through her offer, I desperately needed things. The temptation was too strong.

"Okay," I agreed. "Where are we going?"

"To the small villages," she had planned. We bought garden furniture, lawnmowers and many household things, until fear got the better of me. Being deceitful to provide for my household, did not make me feel good. So I thanked Hayley for helping me, and resigned from this deceit.

My Mum soon raised her concerns about me.

"She's not the same Fiona," she told a friend of mine. "She used to be so sweet."

Mum was now in torment. She said she could not sleep at night because she was so worried that Nigel would kill me. Natasha was also concerned about me.

"You've changed, are you on drugs?" she asked me.

"No I'm not," I answered in defense of myself. I did not want my family to know about the things I was doing. I was ashamed of myself.

Life continued to be tough with the violence in the neighbourhood growing. Everyone became hostile towards one another. Once, a neighbour cut short a drug deal, to the people she was selling to, so they burgled her house. My neighbour and her friends kidnapped the main burglar and tortured him. They stabbed out cigarettes on his skin, hammered his hands, and punctured one of his lungs. Life became sickening as I became caught up in a world of darkness.

The last straw for me was when Hayley and the neighbour on the other side of me were in dispute. One burnt the others fence down, then the other plunged a plug in the other ones head, and so it went on and on.

The atmosphere affected Rueben, and at the age of twelve, he was arrested for a crime he had committed when he was eleven. He had driven some lorries behind a car sale site with some of his friends, causing thousands of pounds worth of damage. Because of his age, the police let him off with a warning. My first baby was growing up and needed some direction. I needed to change my life, fast. I had neglected my children. I had not given them the love and attention they needed and deserved. I was too busy pleasing myself and pleasing others. I took one look at my house and my situation; it was appalling. There were hardly any doors left hanging in the house, and the ones that were there, were either split or in half, due to Nigel. There were holes in the walls. The furniture was filthy. My home was like a barn. It was disgusting. I was now society's reject.

The normal people in society did not look my way. Staring at my bible on my dressing table, my mind told me the answers to life was within the pages. Opening it up, I began to read. I did not understand the words. It was like reading a foreign language, but it gave me comfort to read. I was ready to get out of this life and step into a new one. Closing my eyes, I decided to pray. Suddenly, a vision appeared of a tunnel. I could see a light at the end of it. I knew then, that I was going to be safe. I was going to be taken from my life of darkness, into this bright light.

My new glimmer of hope, gave me a new insight. I could now put everything into perspective. I decided to detach myself from Nigel in as many ways as I could. I would not sleep with him, and would only speak to him when necessary; in order to break the emotional ties and the hold he had on me. This worked because it gave me a new focus on myself, and my future with the children, and not on him. I was now in control.

During this time, the most extraordinary thing happened to me. It was around eleven o'clock at night when I decided to go to bed; I left Nigel downstairs as usual watching television. As I settled down to go to sleep, I felt that aliens were trying to communicate with me. I could sense an electronic wave trying to force itself into my mind. I felt a sudden fear; because I believed I was psychic, I thought I would pick something up, if I allowed it into my mind. This I did not want to happen. Whatever it was, I knew it was evil and felt wrong. Running down the stairs in a panic, I informed Nigel about what had just happened.

"Nigel!" I said my voice shaking. "I think aliens are trying to communicate with me."

"Now you're having a laugh I know you pick things up, but that's a joke."

Although he did not believe me, I knew what I had experienced was not my imagination.

The next day I told one of my neighbours who believed me because of an experience she'd had that same night. In her sleep she felt she was awake. She said, something was trying to whiz her off into space, and she tried to grab hold of her son to protect him from what it was. Suddenly she felt herself being taken far up to a room. She told me a bright light was coming from the room, and something strange was standing behind the door which scared her. Then she felt released from the situation. Convinced by her story, I went round to Sandra's, confused, to tell her. She would believe me, I thought.

"Sandra, guess what? Last night whilst I was in bed, aliens tried to communicate with me." Sandra looked at me expressionless and made no comment.

"Do you want some coffee?" She asked casually, putting the kettle on. Disappointed, for the first time I sensed, she did not believe what I was saying.

I had no evidence of what had happened, until two weeks later, when I had three witnesses. We had all decided to have a night out; Sandra, Martin and one of Sandra's son's, his friend and me. At the end of the night, we all went back to Dee's house for a drink. By the time I was ready to go home, it was around five thirty in the morning.

"I'll drop you home," Martin offered.

"Yeah, I'll come," Sandra's son said.

We all set off, and were just cruising along when I saw a strange light in the sky, just hanging with three other rays of light coming from it.

"What's that?" I asked them, pointing up to the sky.

"Where?" Martin asked. "I can't see what you're talking about."

As we drew nearer they could all see what I was seeing.

"Yeah look! I can see it! Look up there." Martin pointed out to everyone.

"Oh yeah," confirmed Sandra's son.
His friend had fallen asleep and could not be woken up. It seemed to know, we had all seen it, and began to come down lower and lower. As we reached the end of the road and turned the corner, we saw a huge camouflaged object, blending in with the sky and the trees. The world appeared to have stood still. There were no birds, no wind and no sound. Martin got out off the car to double check if what we were seeing was real. To him, it was. Driving further down the road, reaching the next turning, it appeared as though this thing was following us.

"No! It's coming for us!" I shrieked, covering up my face to hide from it.
I don't know what happened next, all I remember is Martin saying; 'look at that.' I was now picking at my nails, trance like. I looked up through the windscreen of the car to see a black object. It was going up and up and up into the distance. It got smaller and smaller, looking like a black hole, until it finally disappeared. It was a bright morning with clear sky, so what we had seen, we knew was real.

A couple of weeks later, someone told me, they heard news on the radio, that some people living near Cambridge, had reported strange sightings of unidentifiable objects. UFO's! One good result from this, was Nigel and Sandra believed me about the communicating with alien's incident. I was not going mad. I tried to look in the bible for the answers of this experience, but as usual, I did not understand anything. I persevered but nothing made sense.

As I became obsessed with U.F.O's, determined to find an explanation to what I had seen, Nigel became angry with me.

"F.....the bible," he stormed one day, grabbing the Bible from my hands, throwing it across the bedroom.

"That's it... it's a curse to do that, you'll see, you'll be punished," I exclaimed.

Three days later, I felt a strong feeling about Nigel.

"You're going to get into trouble in about two weeks time, and not know how to get out of it," I told him.

"Don't be silly nothing can happen to me."

Two weeks later, I got a phone call in the night.

"Nigel's been locked up and kept on remand," Martin told me. My prediction, had come to pass.
Nigel had threatened Caroline's next-door neighbour with a knife in front of her children, because her visitors had called him a black bastard. Although he retaliated because of the racism, as far as I was concerned, he deserved what was coming to him. I knew what it was like to be scared of him. Plus he could not hide the fact he was still seeing Caroline behind my back. I despised him for this. Luckily for Nigel, he was eventually released on bail, and was put on probation for six months.

I was soon offered a bigger house, as with six children we were now obviously overcrowded, living in a three bed roomed house. The house was on other side of town, and was not yet built. It would be ready in six months times. When the plan for the house arrived through the post, I could not believe it. It would consist of three floors, five bedrooms and three bathrooms. Everything was laid on a plate. I had the choice of colours for the decor and carpets. This was my opportunity of a new life. I believed, this was the light at the end of the tunnel I'd seen. However, there was one problem, Caroline lived that side of town.

"She'd better make sure she leaves," I threatened Nigel. He knew her life would be hell with me living there, and so would his. I had been to her house in the past, threatening her, on several occasions. But she just would not give up, and leave Nigel. Nigel warned her about my threats. She packed and left for the other side of Cambridge.

Although I was full of hope of a bright future, in my new home, I became paranoid about my health. After looking through several medical books, I began to believe, I had cancer of the bowels. To me, I was dying and no one could convince me otherwise. I feared that I would die and never have the chance to live in my new home. For once, something good was happening in my life. I believed it would be snatched away, without me having a chance to enjoy it.

"Sit down," the doctor said, offering me a seat.

"This is my twin sister." I introduced, Natasha.

"Hello." The doctor greeted her.

"Right what can I do for you?"

"Well," Natasha began, pausing. "She thinks she's got cancer."

The doctor looked at me smiling.

"I know I have. I get really bad stomach aches," I told him.

"It's unlikely that you have, but I'll examine you anyway." My doctor was used to me believing something was wrong with me.

After a thorough examination, the doctor said I could go home, and that everything was okay. This incident was repeated several times, until eventually, my doctor sent me to the hospital, to have a full examination to put my mind at ease. The x-rays showed nothing was wrong. Thank God!

In the post, a letter arrived. It was about my move, confirming the date of my new tenancy. The time had finally come for a fresh start in life. I could not believe it. The house had doors! And smelt clean and fresh. Not like my previous home, which was now looking like a shack. That was it, I decided once and for all, that I would not let the same thing happen to me and the children again. Determined, not to let this house become like my present one, I packed and I moved, along with my six children, leaving my violent partner. Never to look back at that life again.

With God's grace and mercy, I moved house whilst he was sleeping. Nigel literally slept for the whole day, not waking up once. He had taken lots of valium tablets to block out how he was feeling, knowing he was losing me. My Iranian friend, who was always helpful, and my mum assisted me, with the move. We bought carpets for the bedrooms and laid them. These were the only places that needed to be done. The housing association had already laid carpets on the hall stairs and landings. Mum was delighted that I had the chance for change, and helped on the conditions that I would stand by my word. My Iranian friend went backwards and forwards to my old house all day, stacking and cramming everything in her car. The only things left at the house were my settees, washing machine and beds. The bigger items.

At around twelve o'clock that night, Nigel arrived with some cooked chicken. My Iranian friend was still with me and the children were still up.

"You could have told me we were moving. I've brought you some chicken in case you were hungry," was all he could say.

I looked at Nigel, bewildered. How could he think I would allow him to live with me again?

"Be strong," whispered my friend, as she was leaving. She was right I had to be strong.
Breathing in deeply, for some courage, the words flowed out of my mouth.

"It's over. You're not moving in with us," I stated firmly.

"Please, I love you." Nigel's tone was subtle, like always when he wanted his own way. His tactics had always worked, however, this time his luck had run out.

"You're not moving in with us. It's over," I repeated.

"Please, I love you," Nigel claimed again.

Realising I was serious, Nigel begged and begged, crying whilst rocking backwards and forwards on the floor, pleading to get his own way.

"Mum. Can you come here please?" It was Rueben calling me to his room.

"Please mum, don't take him back," he pleaded.

Looking at Rueben in his cosy warm room and the positive atmosphere around me, my inner strength appeared.

"You have nothing to fear," I reassured him. "I'm not going to take him back," I promised.

Nigel continued to rock from side to side crying like a baby. I spared him no mercy this time, and asked him to leave again. He eventually left. Rejected and defeated.

However, the next morning he returned.

"Can I wash my face? I've slept in my car all night watching the house," he said in a sulk.

I let him wash his face and escorted him through the front door. He was now on my territory, not mine and his. I was in charge now. There was nothing else, he could do to me. He had done it all, and now it was over.

Making a stand against Nigel, showed him, he no longer had control over me. Feeling positive, I had now turned my back on the life Nigel had introduced me to. A life I had lived for seven years. A life of drugs, violence, crime, poverty, deceit, and despair. And I had no intentions of turning back now!

PART TWO

THE LIGHT

CHAPTER 15

THE MYSTERY TRAIL BEGINS

My life at my new house could only get better as long as I did not let the same things happen again. I was now thirty one years old with six children and no direction. I now had the chance to put things right in my life. I realised I did not know my children and they did not know me. I had distanced myself from them due to my own selfish emotions. However, they loved me and I loved them. I was determined to keep my promise of not going back to Nigel.

Mum and Dad were also pleased that I had made a stand against Nigel. This time, they believed, I would not go back with him, and encouraged me, that everything was going to be all right. I was pleased to have their approval of my choice of a new life. Having them around again made me feel good. There was a lot to catch up on. Seven years of heartfelt feelings, had torn us apart. However, this was different. I had moved on.

On the other side of the estate lived Natasha. She was now the mother of four children. She had moved into her house, two months before me. Having her nearby meant she would not let me slip. I was pleased to have her there. No matter what I did or what I was going through, she would never forsake me. She craved for me to change my lifestyle, and was glad to assist me in this.

Within a few weeks of moving, my hair began to grow and my eating habits changed. I was now putting on weight to the delight of my mum.

"You look good Fiona," mum smiled.

I had suffered in silence with anorexia for the past few years. Whenever I looked in the mirror, I would see this big person. I was under eight stone and at my age I did not look good to others. To them, my body was underdeveloped. If I ate anything, I would feel as though I'd put on a stone. Feeling full, meant being fat. So I would make myself physically sick by sticking my fingers down my throat. I would feel smaller afterwards and would feel better about how I looked.

By the time a month had gone pass I was more relaxed about life. I was away from my old neighbours and old friends, apart from Sandra who I loved dearly and would see from time to time. Though they were not at any fault, they were all part of my old life. I was afraid of mixing with them, in case I went back into what I had left behind. I gradually stopped taking heavy drugs and only smoked cigarettes and cannabis to help me cope with life. Within weeks my life became fresh and new.

As we settled in our new homes, some people became wary of me and my twin sister. Due to the problem with

Nigel and Caroline's neighbour from the past, me and Natasha had to stick up for each other, and people became afraid, accusing us of threatening behavior and capable of being violent. It was hard shaking off a bad name. All I wanted was peace. I did not want to be the person I had left behind. I really wanted a change and wanted someone to show me how.

I was pleased when a lady who lived on the same road as me, saw me in a different light.

"Hello, my names Maggie. I just thought I'd introduce myself to you," she said, as she approached me in the park.

"Hi," I greeted.

"I hope we can get on," Maggie suggested, smiling, offering her hand in a warm friendly way.

"Of course, nice to meet you," I replied. Pleased to have met someone new.

Maggie later explained that she had had a bad picture of me, but now that she had spoken to me, she saw me as a warm natured person.

It was the end of my first summer in my new home, and I was wondering what to do with my life. I needed something to do and something to focus on. Sitting on my bed staring through the window, I remember thinking how well my new start was going. Nigel was out of my heart and out of my mind. Gazing at the grassy scenery, a vision suddenly appeared in front of me. I could see the word 'scriptures' clearly written in letters as plain as day. Below, was a picture of a treasure chest with gold and silver jewellery, and different types of pearls and gems. There was so many in the chest that they were hanging over the sides. Instantly, I knew the vision was to do with something spiritual, and it had something to do with a key. The key to the hidden treasures.

"I've got to look into scriptures. There's some information in them which no one knows about," I told Sandra. "There's a key to open this treasure chest. It's the answer to life. I've got to find it."

Sandra smiled. She knew whenever I said something like that; there would be some truth in it.

At this time, I also had a dream of a black man. A Rasta man. In the dream, the atmosphere was musty as though it had been raining. I could feel the dampness in the air, even on waking. The Rasta man was a photographer and had a camera hanging around his neck. He was also French. He was after me. I could hear the shuffling of his feet as he edged towards some bushes where I was standing. As he approached me, I ducked down behind the bushes, so that he could not see me. He wanted some vital information from me, believing I was the only person who had it. To my right was a shed with a beam of light shining from it. Inside the shed was a white woman with a typewriter and a pile of books which she had written. This dream and the vision played on my mind. There was a connection. My instincts told me they would come to pass. But when, I did not know. They were for an appointed time.

Despite the vision and the dream, I still craved to find a meaning to my life. I needed a future and wanted to know what I was here for. I became obsessed with the sky, and dependent on my UFO experience, looking for answers to what this world was about. Anything I saw in the sky which looked unusual, I believed were UFO's. I became obsessed telling everyone I knew, about them. No one would listen until one day I bumped into a neighbour.

"Hi yah, my names Sarah," she introduced herself.

As our conversation deepened, Sarah explained she had been through many challenges in her life. Challenges similar to mine. She said when she met with Jesus, her life changed. She had received healing and was delivered from a life of darkness. A life of witchcraft, domestic violence and drugs. At last I had met someone who could understand me.

"It's the end times. God is coming for his world. The stars seem to be hanging low," I told her.

"Oh most Christians believe we're in the last days. It says in the bible about there will be different signs and wonders."

Sarah's response enhanced my belief about the sky and UFO's. She believed me. As far I was concerned, there was something not right about the sky. The moon looked like it was hanging down and was sometimes a bright red. The stars also appeared lower. In my eyes, the sky was definitely not the same anymore.

Meanwhile problems with my immediate neighbours' arose. Their children were racist towards mine, and their parents would not do anything about it. When my children retaliated, I had all sorts of people knocking my door. 'Your children this, your children that,' they would accuse. Slamming the door in their faces, I thought, 'what was the point in arguing if they did not care what their children said to mine?'

"You use knives, but we use guns," I threatened one day after having enough of the racism. I got the reaction I wanted. In all seriousness to protect my children, I would have gone to any lengths, especially after what they had been through. Every area we lived in, we suffered racism. There appeared to be no escape from this evil.

These incidences and my past experience of racism, led to a desire to write a book on black women and their position in western society. I felt stereotyped being black, single, with lots of kids. I felt a need to let those black women who were suffering the same as me, know that they were not alone. I also felt there were not enough projects for the black community in Cambridge. I tried to go back to college part-time to research, on the political and social side of ethnic minorities. This lasted for a little while. I had to give up on my course, and book writing. There was no-one to help me look after the children. They were still very young, and very demanding.

A strong yearning began to stir up inside of me. I wanted to get my identity back in line with my culture. Searching for books to read, I read a book about slavery, a book about my culture and one about a black African woman trying to adjust to this culture. I could relate to all these stories.

The first book, about black people and slavery, written by slaves, taught me of my historical background. I could see where the root of cultural differences, politically and socially, stemmed from. Although physical slavery happened many years ago, I was a victim of that system mentally, due to the mindset of others. A system which is still undergoing change today.

The second book about my culture, gave me an insight into the way some black people from the West Indies lived their lives in England. The life of an underworld class system, fighting for survival. A life I lived myself. Crime appeared to be their only initiative. To me, some black people could not fit into a culture that did not meet their needs. Institutional racism had caused many born in this country to fail. Giving a rise to an underlying feeling of anger and resentment.

The third book about an African woman, told of her story about her life with her African husband when they lived in England. They had several children together. Her husband had being unfaithful to her with white women, (the opposition), causing the breakdown of their marriage. This story reminded me of myself, and the loneliness I felt with Nigel when he would go off, and be unfaithful. The writer described society as a concrete jungle where racism caused isolation. This was true for me. I felt like a prisoner trapped not just in my own home, but also in society. I craved for freedom.

Amongst my own personal needs, economically, socially and politically, I also had the problem of picking up the pieces from my past, in relation to the children. The move had had a positive affect for my daughters emotionally, but not for my son. Rueben became angry with me.

"You don't know what I had to go through," he would shout sometimes.

"Oh, so you're blaming me for being beaten up," I would say.

This situation continued for a few months until I realised I had to break the pattern. To set him free by apologising for what I had put him through.

"Sit down," I told Rueben one day. "I need to talk to you."

"I'm sorry you had to go through what you did. I realise that whilst I was bringing you up, I was growing up myself."
I had to admit, I really did not know how to be a mum. It would take a long time for me to change and grow up. I needed to go through a process to maturity, which was stunted due to the inflictions in my life. I had to accept I still had not grown up yet. I did not know how to be effective in my life.

Soon, my instincts were telling me that Rueben was going to rebel. I could feel something was brewing.

"Can you send a social worker round?" I asked the receptionist at the welfare office. "It's my son; I think he's going to get into trouble. I need help."

I explained everything that had happened in the past, and she agreed to send someone round to visit as soon as possible.

"Everything seems fine to me," declared the social worker.

"You're house is in order and you appear to cope very well. We have priority cases that we have to deal with. I'm sorry we can't help," she announced.

That was that. I was now left to cope again, on my own. The following week at six in the morning, the phone rang. Rueben had not come home.

"Hello, can I speak to Rueben Lynch's mum please," the police officer asked.

"I'm afraid you're son's being arrested for street robbery."

"He's innocent," I cried.

"You need to come down to the station?"

Rueben had been mixing with the wrong crowd of people in our new area. He was big for his age. At thirteen, he was five foot nine and big built. A lot of people would often mistake him for an eighteen year old, including the police.

After a long interview, Rueben was to be kept on remand for the weekend, charged with street robbery. On the first night I was physically sick. As my heart and soul cried up to the heavens, it was as though, my baby had died. I could hear the world tormenting me once again, as I was faced with another fight for emotional survival. Fortunately the charges were eventually dropped to affray, and Rueben got off with probation. This incident was the beginning of many, and I blamed myself. Why did I not leave Nigel when he first beat me? My sins and the seeds I had sown, had fallen on my child.

Over the next two years, through to the next chapter of my life, most of my spare time was spent at the police station, or at the magistrate's court. It seemed to me, some of the police were determined, they were going to get Rueben for something. Once they chased after him with police cars and a helicopter. He had bumped into a friend in the centre of Cambridge, who had been shoplifting. Whilst speaking to him unaware of the situation, the police arrived. They wanted to question Rueben for speaking to this friend. Through fear of a false accusation, Rueben ran. Later, he was charge with resisting arrest.

There were many more incidences like this. The police finally left him alone after they had beaten him up. I was peacefully sitting at home when one of his friends came running in to tell me what had happened. He was terrified... in so much shock, the colour of his face was pasty white.

"He hadn't done anything wrong," his friend told me.

The police had taken things too far this time. When I arrived at the station, the lies were just flying out of their mouths. They said he had attacked them first. Although there were witnesses, the police did not care; it saddened me to know that my child was suffering at the hands of the law. If the law was not on your side, what chance have you got?

A year after moving, I was on my way to the shops when I met up with my cousin Diane; we started to talk about dreams and visions, and I shared with her the dream I had of the Rasta man. The dream had begun to plague my mind, and I was feeling confused about it. I could not see where it fitted into my life. Diane understood about the dream, as she had many herself. She spoke about horoscopes, and spiritual experiences, which I understood and agreed with.

Diane and I were intrigued by what each other had to say, so we made plans to meet up at my house later that day. We spoke about aliens and my experience, life after death, reincarnation, past lives, all sorts of things of the spiritual world. She told me about the books she was reading, and said I could borrow them.

One was about a medium, giving me, explanatory answers of life after death. The woman gave people messages from their loved ones who had died. The other book, was about angels as spirit guides and the author's life as an automatic writer. She said she would automatically, write down things that these guides would tell her. The guides were supposedly, people from her past life, such as an old loved one or a teacher. Their main message was love. The author gave an example of how she dealt with a neighbour who was always rude to her. Instead of responding negatively she showed her love and it worked. The situation was solved. They became friends. The message I got from both books was that there is life after death and guiding angels.

Diane's and my views on spirituality, led to a deep obsession with the spiritual world. Relying on horoscopes, the reading of cards, spiritual books, oracles and spirits to tell us our future, we had a new hope. A hope that we would somehow get the answers about life and it's meaning.

CHAPTER 16

THE MAN IN MY DREAM

By the end of the school summer holidays, that year, I'd had enough mentally. I had been trapped in the house with the children, and was desperate for a break.

"I need to get away," I pleaded on the phone to Nigel. "Please have them. Just for the weekend," I begged.

I'd hardly seen Nigel since our split, but was prepared for him to have the children at my house, just so I could get away. Nigel agreed whilst I went to Sandra's for the weekend.

At Sandra's I found sanctuary in her bedroom. Because of her children, she thought it best for me stay upstairs so that I felt as though I was away from my usual routine. Sandra was good to me. She brought up food and drinks, whilst I chilled out on her bed looking at spiritual magazines. One magazine contained information about love and how you could meet your future partner anywhere, even on the street corner. The subject of love seemed to be appearing in everything I read.

Whilst thinking about what it would mean to actually find true love, my dream about the Rasta man began to play in my heart. I could sense that it was time for the dream to come to pass.

"I can feel it in the air," I told Sandra.

Apprehensive, we had to wait and see! And after reflecting on my life and future, it was time to go home.

On arriving home, Nigel asked if he could stay. Because he had cared for the children, and our relationship was long gone, I agreed. Just for that night.

"Do you want some?" Nigel tempted, showing me a small white crystal.

"Uhm, why not." I don't know why I agreed so quickly. I suppose I was desperate for some comfort.

As he prepared the coke tin for us to smoke the crack, a silent excitement could be felt between us. This was a usual sensation before taking drugs. As we took in turns smoking from the can, away from the children, my past began to haunt me. The life I had walked away from, was now in my present again.

Searching the floor for what we thought was crack, I became afraid; my mind was imagining things that were not there. 'How did I get myself into this again?' I thought. That was the last time I ever took anything like that again. If I had, I knew I would be trapped. I can remember deciding that I would have to go through a process of change to overcome the habit, of taking any class A drugs. The smell, which made my mind believe I wanted it. The moods, I would have to overcome. I had to refocus my mind to positive things, and fight the cravings which would be gone, over a period of time. Even if it took ten years of my life, it would be worth it, rather than a lifetime of pain. However, I continued to smoke a lot of weed. This was my tranquilizer to get me through life.

Waking up the next morning to the phone ringing, my head felt as though someone had hit me with a hammer.

"Do you want to go to Carnival?" Natasha asked. I could hear the excitement in her voice. "We might find a man," she joked.

"If I go, I just want to have a good day out," I told her. I was in no position to have another relationship. "I'll also have to get a babysitter. I'll ask Andrea, and call you back."

"Okay, I'll ask Sandra, if she wants to go as well," Natasha said.

Dialling Andrea's number, I was scared of her response. I hardly ever asked her to baby-sit, and was hoping she would agree.

"Of course, come back when you want," Andrea offered. Brilliant! I could not believe I was going. Nottingham Hill Carnival was held once a year in London at the end of August. It catered for the needs of the black population, and introduced black culture to other people. This was an opportunity for me to have a taste of what I had been missing, during my years with Nigel.

The drive down to London with me, Natasha and Sandra was refreshing. It was years since I felt so free, going out with no one at home, to answer to. And going somewhere, I wanted to go. Not where I had to try to fit in. For once, I felt alive.

At the carnival, we walked around for a few hours, looking at the brightly coloured floats, with brightly dressed performers. We ate freshly cooked Jamaican food, listening to the music. Everywhere was alive. Towards the end of the day, the excitement I had previously felt soon lifted, replaced by a feeling of desolation. Thinking about the things of the past, I could sense, for the first time in my life, that I had some inner potential. The things that I had gone through, had blocked the development of who I was. There was more to me, than what I and other people had judged. I wasn't just Fiona with six children, struggling hopelessly through life. I was a person, who had rights to achieve in life, just like everyone else. But how was I going to be that person. Carnival, certainly was not the place where I would find myself. It was going to take a lot more than just one event, to bring me back to who I really was.

"Let's go home," Natasha spoke, jolting me into reality from my deep thoughts.

Bored and defeated with life, I was ready to go back to my four walls at home. A home where there was familiarity, and security from a world that I felt lost in. We had just crossed the road, heading for Natasha's car, when a black man approached us.

"Stop!" he shouted anxiously. His outstretched arms shielded us from walking on.

"David," the man called out, to a man across the road. Suddenly two Rasta men appeared.

"You're big people, (grown ups), aren't you?" he asked.
The man could tell we were older than we looked. We all appeared very young for our age. Sometimes I was mistaken for being my children's big sister!

"Where you from?" the man spoke, in patois.
Natasha, Sandra and me, looked at each other hesitantly. We did not usually speak to strange men on the streets, but these men seemed different. Different from the men we were used to. The men appeared pleasant and tranquil. So Sandra spoke.

"Cambridge. We're going home now because we're bored."

"Oh, do you want to go to a party tonight?" The man asked.
It had been a long time since Sandra and I had had a man show interest in us. So when we discussed what should we do, Sandra replied confidently.

"Why not."

"It does not start until ten o'clock, let's go to a café," the man suggested.

"Alright," Sandra replied again.
Trusting her wisdom, we went with them.

Turning to follow the men, Natasha walked beside the man that approached us, whilst Sandra and I walked beside the two Rasta men. I could feel the eyes of the one walking beside me, looking me up and down. He was dressed in typical Jamaican attire. Bright multi-coloured shirt, with bright red trousers. His locks hung down to the level of his chin. They were very neat and tidy. He was of dark skin complexion, slim built, and about five foot seven. This man had an unusual aura, about him. This, interested me.

"You must be ready, willing and able to learn," he finally spoke, after a long silence.

The words struck a cord in me. They were the same words that a spirit guide had used, in the book about angels.

"We are never too old to learn," the man continued.

From that moment on, I became intrigued with my new encounter. I believed those words were a signpost. A signpost from God, for me to listen and learn some lessons on life.

"You haven't asked me my name," I told him instinctively, unsure of how to reply, to what he had just said.

"Oh, Sorry. I'm Carl," he replied softly and politely.

"I'm Fiona."

"What a beautiful name," he flattered.

Determined not to be fooled again, I shoved off his compliment.

We soon reached the café which was a few meters down the road, where we all became engrossed in conversation. We all felt relaxed and at ease with one another. We ordered drinks and continued to talk, in pairs at different tables.

"You're cute. How old are you?" Carl asked looking into my face with love in his eyes, smiling with beautiful perfectly shaped teeth.

"Thirty-two. How old are you?" I responded shyly, looking back into his eyes.

"Twenty-four."

"Twenty-four! I can't have anything to do with you; you're far too young for me."

"What's age got to do with it?" Carl asked smoothly, without reacting to my response.

"A lot!" I snapped back

"Well age is just a number," he insisted.

Thinking our age differences through, maybe, Carl was right; he seemed very mature for his age, like most people from the West Indies. They seemed to grow up quicker, and knew more about life and survival at an earlier age. Besides, I kind of liked him! I was flattered at being chatted up, by someone a lot younger than me.

"Do you have children?" Carl asked. I was a bit worried about what his response would be. Thinking about it, I answered defensively.

"Yes, I've got six."

Waiting for his reaction, my eyes examined him for any signs of disappointment, but there was none. Carl continued smiling, sensing the barrier that I had put up.

"What's wrong, are you ashamed?" he asked.

"No. If a man cannot accept my children then he does not accept me."

Looking into his face, I could see the glint of love, was still in Carl's eyes. After more chat, which then turned into laughter, we all agreed to go to their uncle's place, where Carl and his Rasta friend lived, before going to the party.

On the way to their uncles, we all swapped information about ourselves. Carl and his Rasta friend, had arrived in England the previous month. The other man was born, and brought up in England.

"Do you speak French?" Carl asked me.

"Yeah!" I responded excitingly. "Parlez vous Francais? Bonjour," I joked.

Carl did not respond. Just sat quietly, thinking. I never thought any more about it. Eventually we arrived at the flat to discover a friendly uncle who welcomed us warmly. It was as though we already knew him too.

About ten minutes later, Carl called me to one side.

"Do you know who this is?" he asked pointing to picture of a black man on a white horse.

"No."

I had not seen this person before.

"This is who I worship, Haile Selassie. He is the Almighty. The earth's rightful ruler," he claimed seriously without any doubts.

Taken aback by what he was saying, I made no judgement out of respect. I knew a little bit about Rasta's but not the depths of it.

"He is the 'King of Kings and Lord of Lords, conquering Lion of the Tribe of Judah, a descendent of King David," Carl further claimed.

"That's good you have faith," I finally responded after pausing to look at the picture. I was finding it hard to look at a picture of a man, and think of him as God. Plus I did not know who King David was.

"You're going to meet a Rasta man and put locks in your hair," he prophesied.

"Am I?" I looked at him curiously believing what he was saying. I was so naïve I would believe anything.
After further silence, Carl spoke again.

"I could be talking about me," he concluded looking into my eyes. Pausing once again, waiting for my response.

"You like me don't you?" he insisted

"I don't know you."
I could see the disappointment in his eyes.

"I suppose you're alright," I continued, to make him feel better.

"Do you work?" he asked.

"No, I'm on welfare benefits."

"Have you ever taken cocaine?" This question sent a searing jolt to my body. 'How could I tell him?' 'Why was he asking?'

"No," I lied. The Rasta's I had known in the past had high principals and morals, so I assumed Carl was the same.

"Are you sure?" he asked again.
Pausing to think before I replied, I calculated my words.

"I'm not stupid you know. I do have six kids to look after."

"You're smart. Here's my number, and make sure you call me," he finally concluded.

We swapped numbers and went back to join the others in the other room. By now, I was in a bubble. The night was going the way fate wanted it to.

Entering the club, I could hear the familiar sound of reggae music blasting out of the heavy based speakers. With the smoky atmosphere smelling of marijuana, I was glad to be there. This was my roots. Natasha, Sandra, and I, and our three companions were like three couples who knew each other in a special kind of way. None of us could work it out. The atmosphere of the whole night seemed strange and we all felt it. Carl and I danced together and spoke together as our souls connected.

"This is my kind of music," Carl pointed out. It was a song about Haile Selassie.

I did not care what music was played. Carl made me feel wanted. At the end of the night, we arranged to meet up again the following evening. Something was definitely in the making.

The next evening soon arrived. I had begged Andrea to baby-sit again. As far as I was concerned, this was an emergency. I was not just intrigued by Carl, but also enthralled. He was different from any of my previous partners. He was cultural and spiritual, and I believed I could learn from him about who I was and the meaning of life spiritually.

At the flat, Carl took me to his room. Sitting quietly and shyly on his bed, my eyes wondered around taking in the details of the décor and accessories. Most of the colours in the room were red, gold and green. I was already familiar with these colours of the Rasta culture, but did not know what they meant.

"You alright?" Carl asked gently. He could tell I was nervous.

"Yes thanks," I replied bashfully.

"Why have you come to England?" I questioned, trying to make conversation.

"To study."

"Oh, what are you studying?"

"Journalism?" The word was familiar.

In front of me was a camera, hanging on the wardrobe door.

"Is that why you have a camera?" I asked pointing to it.

"Yeah, yeah," Carl replied, smiling.

A strange wave then came over me. My dream! Looking at Carl, I was amazed and scared at the same time. He looked exactly like the man I had dreamt of. Thoughts of our conversation flashed through my head. He had asked me if I spoke French, in my dream he was French, and when I asked him what he wanted to be, he said a journalist. He had a camera like the one in my dream. An old fashioned one. As I looked around the room, everything fell into place.

"Oh no!" I exclaimed putting my hand over my mouth. "I dreamt of you last year."

Carl smiled as I went on to explain the whole scenario.

"You dream well," he commented. He never asked any questions about it, and the subject was closed. For me I knew God was trying to tell me something, so I decided to follow Carl's lead with an open mind and an open heart.

"I've bought you something. You're my princess and I want to program you to think like me," Carl told me.

I was thrilled. Me a princess and someone like Carl, wanting me to be like them. Nobody had ever held me in esteem like this before, especially someone as strong minded as Carl.

"Turn around, let me put this on for you," he whispered.

It was a necklace made with red, gold, green and black beads; as he put the necklace around my neck he went on to explain what the colours represented.

"Red is for our blood. Gold is for wealth and riches. Green is for peace and love, and black for the colour of our skin."

Carl further explained that green was his favourite colour, which he mainly wore. He said if he wasn't wearing green, he would wear one of the others.

He taught me a bit more about what he believed in. I had never had anyone explain about Rastafarianism like this before. Carl explained that Haile Selassie's wife, Princess Menen, was the Queen of heaven.

"I didn't know there was a queen of heaven."

"Yeah" Carl was happy. He had caught my attention.

"Why? Is she like mother nature?"

"Yeah, yeah. That's right," Carl responded. Pleased with my definition.

"Haile Selassie, a black Ethiopian king, was crowned 'King of King's, Lord of Lord's, conquering Lion of the Tribe of Judah' in July 1930," he told me. "Look!" Carl went on to show me in the book of Revelation in the Bible, (chapter 19 verse 16), the words KING OF KINGS AND LORD OF LORDS to give definition to his explanation of how Haile Selassie was God.

"See. Look. Haile Selassie was crowned this," he affirmed again.

Although what he was saying sounded right, I could not feel any spiritual connection.

Going through the bible, Carl further explained that Haile Selassie was the rider on the white horse as stated in the book of Revelation chapter 6 verse 2, like in the picture he had shown me. This meant nothing to me but words and a picture.

"So, erm, what about Jesus," I asked.

"A white man," Carl emphasized defiantly.

I did not question him any further, he was adamant. Jesus meant nothing to him. Besides, I could relate to what he was saying because I had this image myself, that Jesus was white. But something inside me, made me feel, that Jesus was relevant in some way.

"There is no God! My mum's a Christian, and I burnt everything to do with Jesus in her house. There is only the

Almighty. Haile Selassie is the Almighty," Carl asserted crossly. "All the things around you, including material things, like computers and TV's, are gods."

What he said made sense. There could only be an Almighty, and not lots of different gods. Jesus being one of them.

Further on in our conversation, I realised Carl was totally against white people because of the times of slavery. He believed that black people were the chosen ones. He had decided to come to England, to take back what he said belonged to the black race from the times of slavery. He also saw, the building up of western society, in the post-war period by black Caribbean's, as their rightful possession. I thought he must be right. Since we, as black people were the minority, and were seen as different from other cultures, we must be God's chosen people. Carl had the black versus white attitude. By the end of that night, I adopted this attitude. I believed I could do anything I wanted, and get away with it. I was God's child, and white people weren't. They had robbed me of my life, and now I would take back the things they had taken from me, and my ancestors. I now had everything in perspective. Carl had succeeded, in some way, in programming me into thinking like him.

The next day I questioned Sandra intensely, about the things that Carl had told me.

"He said Princess Menen was the Queen of Heaven. Is that right?" I asked her.

"Yep. The moon represents Princess Menen, and the sun represents Haile Selassie," Sandra explained.

I found this concept strange, looking at the moon and sun as people, but accepted Sandra's explanation.

"I love you," Carl told me on my next meeting with him at my house. He had met all my children and liked them. I found this unbelievable. How could someone fall in love so quick and accept my situation so easily? Then I remembered what I had read in the magazine at Sandra's house, about meeting love anywhere, even on the streets, so it was possible. My destiny was already designed for me.

"You love me, don't you," he further insisted.

"I don't know you, but I do love you. Its universal love," I replied, hoping Carl would accept my answer.

Smiling, Carl asked another question. An unexpected one.

"Will you marry me?" he proposed, still smiling.

Looking into his eyes, I feared a hidden agenda.

"Why do you want to marry me? Is it for love, or just so you can get your stay here?" I was not going to be fooled. Not after all the things I had suffered.

"Both reasons," he replied. "I love you and to get residency I have to either be married, or attend college."

I was not convinced, and was determined this time I was not going to be used again. Carl had to prove that he loved me.

"Well go to college then.," I stated... which he did. Not to study journalism, but to study computers at a college in London near where he lived.

Because of the attention Carl showed me, I soon became obsessed with him. I would phone him at every opportunity. Sometimes up to five times a day. Not giving him the chance to phone me. He would always speak to me, although he had problems hearing what I was saying. My weakness had shone through. The damage of the past had made me dysfunctional. My speech and attitude, could not hide the way I really was. Although I was a quiet person, the suppression over the years had affected me a lot more than I thought. Carl was now about to bring everything out into the open.

"I can't hear you," he'd say.

He was not the first person to say this to me. The volume of my voice was very low. It was not in my power to turn it up.

"I'm having to see if there is anything on the phone to turn up the volume, are you on something?" He would ask.

"No, I've just been through a lot." I would tell him.

If only he knew. The effects of taking drugs, had had a negative affect on who I was, along with all the trauma I had suffered.

"Why are you like that?"

"Like what?" I asked.

"You're not doing anything with yourself and you seem... seem a bit."

"Seem a bit what?" I interrupted, in a mood. The man I'd fallen for was now making me feel insecure. There was no hiding of who I had become from Carl. He was seeing all the downsides of my life. The criticism's, that's how I saw them, soon became more regular.

"Too many people in Britain are on benefits, you need to work," he commented.

Feeling shunned by his words, I knew he was right. I had lived my life, plodding along with no goals or self respect. I'd allowed others to dictate my life for me.

"You must have a dream. Even if it's of having a jet plane. It doesn't matter how big it is." Carl continued to preach. "You deserve the best."

"You're right," I answered, thinking about what he was saying. Never in my life had I dreamt of having anything until now. Carl encouraged me to have an aim. I was worthy of having bigger things. He wasn't putting me down after all.

"I want a house in Jamaica. Somewhere for me and my children to run to, in case this country does not want us here anymore," I told him.

It felt a bit scary announcing that I wanted to do something. That I had a dream to achieve something, even though it was not appropriate in my circumstances.

"That's what I want too," Carl confessed. "Since you live here, you will probably know what to do," he continued.

Carl had now put me in a predicament. He believed in me. That I knew what to do and how to do it. If only he know. I didn't. I had to think quickly. I needed to get a job fast, and start making constructive plans to achieve our goal of our home in Jamaica.

Challenged, I did not want to be put to shame. But, what about the children? I was living on my own with six, and no help. How could I possibly achieve anything like this? The pressure was on. I was not strong enough to take on such a big project.

I began to feel inferior and inadequate around Carl. Especially when everyone else was around. The two people closest to me were self sufficient, and I was not. Natasha worked as a legal secretary, so this gave her the confidence she needed to be herself. Sandra had money. She would provide not just for herself and her partner, but also for me and mine. I would feel belittled in front of everyone, as it was obvious, that I did not have any of my own resources and I was reliant on her. I could not tell Sandra not to help me in their sight, due to my insecurities as I still lacked the confidence to speak up.

Because of doubts about myself and where I was in life, I began to feel like Cinderella. I believed they were looked upon as being more worthy than me, because of their outward appearance and confidence, shattering my self esteem even more. I had no nice clothes, and would have to make do. I was the reject of the crowd, with a lot of issues.

Reminiscing, I began to feel resentful about my friends from the past. I had previously babysat many times for them to go to work, but no one would do it for me. I was like everyone's slave. I would cook, clean and entertain them and their children. I always wondered if anyone even noticed me. I thought if I died would they notice that I did not exist anymore. Never mind, maybe the problem was me. Why could I not just say no, to people? Why did I always say yes? Leaving myself no room to do anything.

Feeling as though something was wrong with me, I began to feel saddened, remembering how people had made me out to be unintelligent, even though I went to college.

"Natasha's the bright twin, Fiona's the quiet one," I remembered them saying.

"Oh Fiona you don't know what you're talking about," they would say if I said anything, or contributed to a conversation.

These comments started from an early age.

I decided to share my feelings with Carl and the story of my abusive pass of domestic violence. I hoped he would understand why I had become so dysfunctional, but he only became stricter with me. He showed no empathy what so ever.

"Has everyone always been like that with you?" he enquired with his usual Jamaican accent.

"Yes, but a lot more since I was with Nigel," I explained.

"Well get used to it. Everyone should learn to love one another." How could I argue with what Carl had said? He was right, we should all love one another. 'You can't change people, but you can change yourself,' I thought.

Because Carl was different from any one I had been out with before, I was desperate to stay with him, and learn about myself personally and culturally all over again. Until one day without warning, he had some unexpected news. Carl was about to treat me like everyone else. Stupid!

We had been together nearly four months, and Christmas was approaching, when Carl told me the news.

"There's a girl who likes me. She has three houses and I want to be with her. You're still my woman, just hold a vibe, (meaning be patient)," he told me.

"I know what I'm doing, remember you're still my women, King Solomon had many wives, I plan to get some money out of her then we can live together and sort out our house in Jamaica. Give me three months," he pleaded.

Within months of meeting Carl, he had programmed me to believe what he believed. He had built me up and now he was pulling me down. What had I done wrong? Pride took its place in my heart. There was no way I was going to let a man pull me down again. "Rise above it," I could hear Janet's words echoing through my mind. I must walk tall and never let my guard down. This time if I surrendered to my feelings I was going to fall. Never to get back up again.

Somehow, I knew this girl was not telling him the truth about her riches. I knew it was only a matter of time before she would be exposed. Because of my dream about Carl, I swallowed my pride, and waited patiently for him, believing he had the key to what I was been led to spiritually.

After confiding in Sandra once again about my situation, my mind was put at ease. She explained how poor it can be in Jamaica, if you have no work, as they have no welfare system out there. She said some of them come to England, and they see the things we have here and want the same, to the point of becoming corrupt. The pressures of living in England with no work permit had clearly taken its toll on Carl. He was desperate to have what he had never had before. He was easily led where money was concerned. He saw England as the land of gold and riches thinking every one born and raised here, must have money. He wanted the things that he had been deprived of in Jamaica. Clothes, a nice car, amongst many other things. He did not care how he was going to get them, or who he hurt in the process.

Rasta music, which Sandra introduced me to, became my salvation. As I played the music of a known reggae artist, the words sung in my heart. 'Be strong; hold a firm meditation, one day things must get better'. The words were really encouraging along with 'Jah, (which means God), has put an angel over me'. Meditating on these words gave me a sense of protection and hope for what was to happen next.

CHAPTER 17

THE SPIRITUAL DIMENSION

The New Year arrived, and Carl was still on my mind. In my heart, I knew our relationship was not over. God was leading me to something; to the hidden treasures in the vision. I needed the key to unlock it. It was only a matter of time before the mystery would unfold.

In the meantime, I prepared myself for change. Pressurised, I went back to work. I got a job as a mental health care assistant, at a hospital in Cambridge. I wanted to prove to Carl and myself, that I was capable. I was just like everyone else, able to work, and to be independent from the welfare state. Because the twins were three years old, they were not old enough to go to school, so I had to pay for a child minder. More expenses!

Around this time, I had another dream of a light-bulb. It was hanging from a ceiling, shadeless. I realised, in waking, it was another clue to the mystery trail that I was on. But what did it mean? I would find out later.

I was just getting used to the idea of waiting for Carl when the phone rang late in the night.

"Ello." The familiar voice did not surprise me.

"So what, you can't phone?" Carl questioned.

"I've been busy," I lied.

"I want to come to Cambridge to live with you."

"What have you done?" I dared to enquire believing something must have happened for him to phone me so late.

"I've just bust up that girls head," he told me.

Carl found out she had lied to him, and now he wanted to come running back to me. A part of me was glad about what had happened. The woman as far as I was concerned, had not cared about my feelings, so I had no sympathy for her. Brushing aside what Carl had confessed to, my thoughts focused on living with him. As much as I wanted him to come and be with me, there was a block. I was not emotionally able, or strong enough, to handle his ways. The food he ate and his lifestyle was totally different from mine. I was not the person I used to be. I could now see how much of Nigel's ways and lifestyle I had adopted. I was damaged goods. I was weak. I would never be able to keep up with Carl, and his demands.

My financial situation was also not good. I still struggled greatly. Because Carl, could not go to work due to legal reasons, I would have to look after him. After weighing up the odds, I had to be honest with myself, and with him. Living with Carl, would be impossible. After putting the phone down, I decided to write him a letter explaining my situation.

"How does food sell in Cambridge? I want to be with you," Carl inquired after receiving my letter.

"What sort of food?" I questioned, stunned by the fact he wanted me. To make things work out.

"Fish and chips."

"Quite well, English people like that sort of thing, its one of their traditional dishes," I told him.

"Why don't we set one up... a fish and chips shop," he suggested.

'What a good idea,' I thought. But if only Carl knew, it was out of our means.

"I've got a better idea, what about a food van business selling fast food," I suggested, (without remembering what the man at the psychic fair had told me).

Carl liked my idea. We agreed that he would live with me once I was settled in my job.

Enthusiastic for out dream to work out, I set out on this mission. I sought a business adviser who gave me all the details I needed. I calculated, that if I worked hard for three months at the hospital, I could make the money to start the business. Carl could then move in with me. He could help me run the business, giving us the income we needed. I had it all worked out, and Carl agreed to it all. With Carl on my side and his teachings on the Rastafarian faith, I began to seek to know his God with a willing heart. I occasionally wrapped my hair, as a statement of belief.

I began to feel a bit more included, in the system of society in regards to work. Some of the feelings of worthlessness, that I had felt, soon began to lift. Excited, I told everyone about my business project, and my future plans, but no one showed any interest. In fact, no-one wanted to even listen to me about anything I said. I suppose they did not take me seriously. Frustrated with everyone for their lack of attention towards me, I began to take these issues out on Carl.

"What's wrong with you?" he would ask picking up on my mood.

"Nothing, I'm fed up," I would tell him. I just did not know how to speak up without being defensive.

"So you're throwing it all on me," Carl would say.
It was true. Carl became the dart board for my problems and emotions. I loved him very much for the attention and care he gave me, but I could not hold back how I was feeling. Our relationship began to suffer.

After confiding in Diane about all that I'd gone through, she told me about the person I used to be.

"I remember how you once were," she said. "You were stronger and well organised. I'm not going to be happy, until you get to the place where you were before. You used to make decisions for yourself; you had order in your life. I know you're tough, because of what you've been through, but you're not there yet."

Encouraged by her words on one hand, but on the other discouraged, 'why doesn't she help me?' I thought.

Considering what I had been through, and now with six young children who needed to be looked after, I believed, I was doing a good job. So any comments in regards to my situation, would make me feel put down, even if they were positive.

Things soon came to a head for me emotionally. I began to resent not being able to speak up for myself. Whenever Natasha was around she would be my spokeswoman. This would agitate Carl. It showed up my inadequacy to communicate, giving him more ammunition to make me feel as though something was wrong with me. I just wished I could be normal. My natural insecurities and the things I had gone through, were now a stumbling block to me.

I also felt Sandra had betrayed me, by hiding things from me. One time a male cousin of her's, had befriended Carl and his friend. They wanted to get a large quantity of weed to sell. Sandra knew, I did not want Carl involved in anything like that. If he got caught he would get deported; so she hid this plan from me. When I heard about it, she got nasty with me, saying she had known about it for a month. Upset, I kept quiet about my feelings towards her, questioning myself, why could I not just speak up? What was my purpose for being here?

Anxious to find answers, Beverly came to mind. I now know it was God, who had planted the thought of her there. I had not seen her for years, and after all that had happened, I did not want to see her again. Beverly was seriously into Rastafarianism, and I needed to know more about it, for my own sake. I needed to know God, and wanted to understand Carl's way of thinking. Spiritually driven, I was compelled to go and see her; so with a sense of urgency I paid her a visit.

On the way to Beverly's there was a van parked around the corner, on it was a picture of a light bulb. It triggered the memory of my dream. This was to be, a significant sign in my spiritual course. As I approached her house, I could feel a presence in the air. Taking a deep breath, I knocked the door. Beverly greeted me, with much warmth and love.

"Hi," she smiled, as though she was expecting me.
Suddenly the tears flooded from my eyes. I could not stop crying. I had had enough of life and my emotions were overflowing.

"Ah, what's wrong?" she questioned.

"Nobody likes me," I cried, spluttering.

"Don't let anyone make you cry." She spoke softly, twiddling the plaits in my hair affectionately.
Comforted by her welcome, I went on to explain what had been going on in my life, and how I was now feeling. I did not tell her about Carl and the woman, but asked her about King Solomon in regards to Rasta's having many wives.

"Some Rasta's do have several women. They have their main woman who they call their wife, and other women, who are their mistresses," she explained.

"But in these days there's all sort of diseases," I told her.

"I know."

"Would you let your man have more than one woman?"

"No way, I'd leave him."

Beverly continued to talk about Rastafarianism and said it was her life. She said, if it was not for her belief in this, she would not be here. It helped her to get through her troubles. Her house was a shrine for Haile Selassie. There were pictures of him everywhere. One of them, stood out to me. It was a picture of him signing a piece of paper. Looking at him, I tried to relate to him as being God, but it just did not seem right. To me, he was just a man.

Beverly went on to explain that she belonged to a group of Rasta's named Israel. A twelve-tribe movement, where each person would be given a name for the month in which they were born. For example, if you were born in March, you would be called Benjamin. She said they believed that Jesus was God's son, and that Haile Selassie was the next manifestation of God, but not God himself. These beliefs were different from what Carl had taught me.

"Carl said he's burnt Jesus," I told her.

"What! You can't acknowledge the father without acknowledging the son," she explained. "It says in the bible no one should add, or take away from it otherwise they'll be cursed. There's the beginning, the middle and the end. That's why I don't agree with them type of Rasta's. They come over here to get what they want, and don't care what they do, to get it. They're all about money. That's why I'm surprised he's with you, you've got six children, live in Cambridge, and have nothing," she went on. "Plus the type of Rasta, Carl says he is, wouldn't come to England. He would stay in Jamaica and live in a bush."

"He has," I confirmed. Carl had once told me he lived in a bush for several weeks. I did find this odd at the time, but it was his belief, so I respected it.

"He must be different from the rest... a true Rasta," Beverly claimed.

"So I should be lucky then to be with him, and shouldn't be horrible?" I questioned Beverly, believing he must love me despite my situation.

"Yes in the time of Jesus, they persecuted the messenger."

In my confusion, I now believed Carl was a messenger just like Jesus, telling me the word of God, so I rushed to London, to see him the next day. I told him I was sorry for being horrible, and pleaded for his forgiveness. I wanted to do everything right in the sight of God.

After sorting things out with Carl, we got on better. My thirty third birthday arrived, and we decided to spend the day together at my house with Natasha and her children. Carl cooked a nice dinner, at my expense as usual, though I didn't mind. I was just glad to have him around. He did not buy me a present but gave me a birthday card. Inside he had written that he loved me, which was good enough for me. At least I had some acknowledgement.

Settling down for the evening, he explained about how he was free from his past.

"I've been given a clean piece of paper, my sins have been forgiven. So can yours," he claimed.

"How?" I questioned. I did not understand what sins I had, and if I had any, how I could be forgiven.

"Through the holy trinity," Carl explained, making a triangle shape with his fingers. "Haile Selassie, Bob Marley and Marcus Garvey, they make up the trinity. If you confess your sins to them, you will be forgiven." This confused me even more, but gave me food for thought.

After a good birthday, I not only looked forward to seeing Carl again, but also to hear more information about God.

I found out that Bob Marley was known as a prophet to the black people, even though he was mixed race, and that Marcus Garvey, a Jamaican, had told his people, to 'Look to Africa where a black King shall be crowned, for the day of deliverance is at hand'. Black people needed hope in a society where they were so deprived. With the aftermath of slavery, not only did the countries of the West Indies and Africa need building up, so did the people. When Haile Selassie was crowned King of Kings and Lord of Lords in Ethiopia, he was believed to be the promised deliverer. He appeared to fight for reformation, such as education and health care and equality. It was at this time the Rastafarian movement began in Jamaica, and many believed he was god.

Carl began to stir up guilty feelings in me. Feelings, that I had never felt before. He would make statements that would make me question myself.

"You're hiding things from me," he would say accusingly. Soon, I started to confess to him things about my past, believing that was what he meant. I saw him as pure and clean, because he was religious, and felt I had to tell him the truth.

"I've been involved in drugs," I admitted.
Carl was calm and collective as I confessed.
"What kind?" he questioned.
"Um, weed, cannabis." I didn't dare tell him the whole truth.
Carl was still quiet. Thinking he was waiting for more information, I continued to tell him more.
"Um, also I had an abortion."
"When!?" Carl was unable to contain his surprise.
Struggling to keep calm, I explained to Carl the situation and the reasons why. Feeling better, after telling him about my past, I felt free. Someone knew, and did not judge me for the life I lived and the things I had done.

This feeling of freedom did not last long. Carl had now gained total control over me emotionally. Maybe I shouldn't have been so honest about myself. I remembered, my mum once saying, 'never tell a man everything, they'll use it against you.' Perhaps she was right. Unsure of how Carl felt about me, I began to do whatever he wanted, to please him. I wanted to make myself appear good in he's sight. I believed he was a man of God, and felt I had to respect him. I started to live in total fear, as I sensed a strong spiritual power around him. Thinking, if I did the right thing, I could have it too.

Finding myself at Beverly's again, I searched for more answers.

"How do you know that God is real?" I asked.

"It's just a feeling."

"Do you believe that Princess Menen is to be worshipped?" I asked, remembering what Carl had told me.

"She's dead, so how can you worship someone who's dead?"

Confused, I did find it strange, that God had a wife. However, I wanted the feeling that Beverly and Carl had. After leaving Beverly's, I decided I would search for it myself.

Crying in desperation to be sincerely loved, I decided to call upon the spirit of Haile Selassie by reading Psalm 101. The psalm which Carl had said Haile Selassie had recited on the day of his coronation as king of Ethiopia. Speaking the words, "When will you come unto me," (KJV). I gradually sensed the heavy presence, which I felt Carl had, falling upon me. Feeling the presence within me, elated, I believed, I had found God. Finally finding something personal for myself, that no one could take away from me. Although intrigued, I did not know enough about this spirit I was worshipping.

At the same time, I still believed in having a past life, and life after death, because of the books I had read. False spirits, which I thought were real, were telling me things. Things which appeared to be true. For instance, one morning I woke up with a message for Sandra.

"Anne said don't do it," I told her.

She was amazed. I did not know who Anne was, but she did. Anne was Sandra's mum's sister, who had died.

"I knew it," she said, "My family always treats me like a baby. This time I'm doing what I want."

Because of her response, I thought it was all real. This sort of thing happened on more than one occasion, which enhanced my beliefs.

One day whilst Sandra and I were visiting a male Rasta friend, I saw a picture on the wall of a black Mary holding a black Jesus.

"Jesus was black," he stated. "This picture is a copy of an original found in Ethiopia."

I had my doubts about whether the picture was real or not, but as he went on to explain, I realised Jesus could not have been white. Born in Bethlehem, a Middle East country, he would have been olive skinned or dark skinned. His appearance would have been more multi-cultural. I couldn't wait to tell Carl that Jesus was black, as though I had some new information, to do with God. Carl's view about God was based on colour, and not on the spirit. When I told him he never responded. He kept quiet as though he was in deep thought.

As time went by, I began to see how Carl used his faith towards me. He became manipulative, getting money from me, which I couldn't afford to give him. He would always say he had nothing to eat, and I would feel sorry for him, and would send him money though the post. His attitude confused me. The Rasta's that I had known in the past were peaceful, kind and gentle. They would give and not take from a woman, especially one on her own, with six children.

"Why does he behave like that?" I asked Sandra.

"It's because of his levity," she said. "Don't forget, coming from Jamaica, they have nothing. We have to give alms," she insisted.

I had already given Carl lots of money. He never seemed to have any. Nevertheless, because of what Sandra had said, the compassion in my heart led me to give more. I could not bear the thought of Carl doing without, even though I did not have much myself. He was in a strange country, and according to him he hardly knew anyone. Plus I had known hunger myself, and believed it was the right thing to do, in the sight of God. So amidst my confusion about Carl, I gave him most of what I earned.

Soon I was working nights at the hospital, to keep up with helping Carl, and catering for the needs of my children. The pay was better, so it seemed feasible that I did this. And once again, I did without. In the back of my mind, I knew Carl's demands on me were not right. Always wanting money. But because of my kindness, I would feel a compulsion to give to him at his request, and Carl would happily take it. He had no conscience.

"I'm coming to live with you," Carl soon stated.

Being established in my job, meant we could now fulfill our dreams. I had enough information about the food business; we just needed the money to get it going. My plan of using my wages was long gone; Carl had spoilt it by his begging. Despite this, I was worried about how I would cope with Carl around me all the time. I had to be honest with myself. He was still too strong for me mentally. I did not feel stable enough to look after myself, and my children properly, let alone anyone else. But I couldn't turn back now. I also had too much on my mind. My beliefs about God, the other spiritual things, and my UFO experience confused me. I wondered if I was going mad. I had told the children that there were aliens flying around in the sky in space ships. I would lead them to the front door at night, telling them to wave to them because they were their friends. Everything I saw in the sky, in my eyes was a UFO. Deciding to confide in Carl about this, I put all my trust in him. Surely he would understand, I believed. He was a man of God.

Carl listened carefully agreeing with everything I told him. So I trusted him with more of my beliefs.

"I believe that Haile Selassie is God, and at the end times, he and his army, who are immortal, will come down in space ships for the chosen people," I told him.

"I'm going in that ship," Carl said to my satisfaction. "How big is it?"

I could hardly contain my excitement. Carl understood what I was saying.

"As big as Cambridge."

"As big as Cambridge?" he repeated astonished.

"Yes," I replied with confidence. Glad that I had got his attention.

"Let me get back to you on this. I need to take this in," he spoke after much hesitation.

Believing I had found the key to the hidden treasures, I hurriedly told everyone. I told them that Haile Selassie was God, (the key), the spirits of the dead were angels, and that there was life after death with an immortal body due to the U.F.O and alien experience. To my disappointment, no one believed me. But I didn't care. I had found what I was looking for. God!

Focusing on Haille Selassie as God, I was proud that I had been chosen. But the more I dug deeper, meditating on him, and believing in aliens, the more I became mentally disturbed. My mind felt like it had been taken over, as though it was detached from my head. I soon became afraid. God seemed dark and horrible. I would continuously see in a vision a black army of men, riding on black horses, galloping from space ships that had landed. They were on a mission to take over the world. To kill everyone who did not believe that Haile Selassie was God. If this was what God was about, I thought, I'd rather be dead. Frightened, I tried my hardest not to say, or do anything that might upset, who I thought was God.

About a week after our conversation, Carl got back to me.

"I can't come and live with you," he told me. "I have to go to college."

"I thought we were setting up a business together. What about our house in Jamaica?" I pleaded.

"We'll talk some other time I can't talk right now."
Great... Carl had let me down again. I had worked so hard towards our dreams and our relationship. To make it work. And now he had robbed me of everything. Our future together was now shattered and my heart was torn in two. Had the man at the psychic fair got things wrong, or had I. He did say I would be selling hot dogs, not fish and chips, though the idea of a food van was the same.

Confused and overwhelmed, I did not speak to Carl for a couple of weeks. I did not call him and he did not call me. The tears would not stop flowing. Every step I took in my life, seemed to lead to nothing. Recalling our previous conversation, I realised I must have scared him off. Telling someone I had seen a space ship as big as Cambridge, would have been enough for them to question whether I was stable or not. I had to put things right.

Plucking up the courage, I decided to phone him. Explaining his reasons for not coming to live with me, Carl said it had nothing to do with what I had told him. He said the woman who was responsible for his stay in England was upset, that he was with someone with six children. She said if he came to live with me, she would not sponsor him anymore. Relieved, he did not think I was mad; I gave Carl the benefit of the doubt, and continued to have a relationship with him. I needed him and his teachings, even though he always messed me around.

Carl taught me more about the bible. I began to focus on reading psalms and proverbs.

"They will encourage you," he told me.

Psalms helped me to talk to God about my issues in life and to praise Him. Whereas Proverbs helped me to recognise the principals of life. Basically whatever you sow is what you reap. I could see things more clearly, and felt calmer within myself. But soon, I became disturbed again.

"Something's not right," I told Diane.

"Why do you say that?" she asked, curious at my statement.

"Because my stomachs doing summersaults."

"Maybe you're just worried," Diane pacified.

"No, something's wrong I have to phone Carl up."

"Wait until you've calmed down." Diane encouraged. "It might be your imagination."

"I can't. I had a dream last night that Carl finished with me and when I woke up the feelings seemed real."

"Well have you spoken to him today?"

"Yes, this morning."

"Did you tell him about the dream?"

"Yes, he said that it isn't going to happen. I have to phone him now."

Diane watched as I dialled Carl's number with anticipation. I hated when my instincts spoke to me. There was no escape from what they told me.

"Some girl said she'll have a baby for me," Carl confessed casually, as though he was speaking to a friend. "I knew her in Jamaica, and I want a child," he continued laughing.

"You're not ready to have one; I also need to get my stay in England. This is my only way. We can still be friends."

Distraught, I hung up the phone. Carl had finished with me. He knew I could not have any more children. I had been sterilised after having the twins, and now he was flaunting this fact in my face.

Diane felt sorry for me. Carl was always building up my hopes then letting me down.

"There's a medium fare on tomorrow, apparently this guy who's coming to speak is really good. Do you want to come? You may get some answers," she softly suggested.

Unhesitatingly, I agreed. I needed to make some sense out of this relationship.

At the medium fare, I was told that I was very quiet and needed to speak up. Although it was something I already knew, I believed the message came from my friend who had died when I was about ten years old. No one could have known this except someone who already knew me. I did notice, the man told people a lot of things about their past, but not about their future. He obviously had no insight into this. Nevertheless, the main message for me, was that I must speak up.

In pain without Carl, life became harder for me emotionally. I needed his input, as though I was addicted to him. He would make the pain go away, I believed.

"I can't live without you," I told him.

Carl was enthralled. He now had me where he wanted me. Under his control.

"Am I your woman then?" I dared to ask without mentioning the other woman. I wanted to believe he was not with her.

"You don't have to ask that," he told me.

"Well say it then," I insisted.

"You're my woman. But don't keep calling me."

Disappointed and feeling rejected, I justified Carl's words. I was phoning him up to five times a day. Hounding him, leaning on him, depending on him, to satisfy my emotional needs.

Over a period of time, I became more spiritually confused, as Carl disrespectfully, hurled insults at me once again. If Carl was a man of God, how could he speak to me, and treat me the way he did.

"You're English," he would say in a sharp teasing voice, as if it was wrong to be English.

"I'm not," I would defend.

"What nationality are you then?" he would taunt.

"Jamaican," I would answer.

"Me is an African," he'd say showing off.

Because Haile Selassie was African, Carl would emphasis that he was one too, although he was born in Jamaica. Africa was seen as the root of mankind, and the promised land where all the chosen ones would live one day. If only he knew my struggles. Not knowing who I was culturally or spiritually was not a good place to be in. Continuing to criticise me, his questions became personal.

"Why are you like that? Why do you stand like that?"
The more the insults, the less I spoke, until I could hardly speak to him, or anyone else unless I was totally familiar with them. Even then, it was hard, as no-one listened to me because of my quietness. I'd stare into space with my mind wondering, without knowing it was happening. I was never conscious of doing it. Someone could be speaking to me, and I would not realise. Or I would be in a room full of people, and it would happen. Natasha and Diane once said they had a conversation about me deliberately with me in the room; they even called me names whilst I sat staring into space to see if I could hear them, but I didn't.

A month passed and I had not seen Carl. I continued with my obsession of phoning him up to five times a day. I just could not help it. Hearing Carl's voice on the phone, was like food for my soul.

"You must have the best in life. Learn to drive, have a car, all the nice things," Carl told me.

"Buy some paint. I'll help. I'll paint your hallway for you." I could not believe it, someone was going to help me, and it was Carl. He'd had a change of heart.

Carl came and did a good job of my hallway. As he painted we chatted and shared a few things with each other.

"Oh, you can do the whole house for me!" I joked excitedly.

"I'm only doing it because you helped me," he replied.

So it was like that. Carl was helping as payment for what I had done for him, not because he loved me.

Keeping my feelings to myself, I surrendered to the fact I was flogging a dead horse by being with him. What could I do? Leaving him would be too painful.

"I feel I need to read psalm 118," Carl said before he left for London.

Turning the pages of the bible, Carl began to read.

"It is better to trust in the Lord than to put confidence in princes." He read from verse nine (KJV).

"See... look!" I said. "I shouldn't trust you," I laughed, trying to make light of what I had said.

"It could mean princesses too, you know," Carl voiced softly and continued to read. "The stone *which* the builders refused is become the head *stone* of the corner." (Verse 22 KJV).

"I like that," I admitted. I did not know that this stone was Jesus, but somehow related it to myself.

After Carl had gone, I twisted my hair into little dreadlocks and wrapped it. It was now time for me to have them as a signature of who I was in society, and a sign of who I represented. I had always relaxed my hair to make it nice and straight, and easy to manage. I also changed the way I dressed, from mini-skirts to long dresses and long skirts. I decided once and for all, Rastafarianism was the only way for me.

Despite this decision, I had to admit, I was struggling to keep up with Carl's expectations of me. It was not in me, to be the way he wanted me to be. I needed to grow naturally.

Yielding to this reality, hurt me deeply. It was only a matter of time before I knew we would have to part. For good! What happened next was to take me into another dimension, where I'd never been taken before. I believed I had experienced all things possible in life, but not this. I thought I had already found God, and that everything for me would be alright, but it wasn't. I tried to hold onto Carl, but I knew it was time to let go. My journey with him was over.

I was lying on my bed when I saw the word, 'Almighty,' appear in front of me. 'Do it now,' I heard a voice say. Getting up off the bed in dismay, I heard the voice again. 'Do it now,' it whispered. I knew I had to end the relationship with Carl. I trusted it was God telling me this.

Shaking from head to toe, I dialled Carl's number, scared of what I was about to do. I loved him very much, and didn't know how I was going to live without him. But I had to put my trust completely in God.

"I'm taking myself out of this," I bravely told him.

"What you say? You're taking yourself out of this?" Carl stuttered, as he repeated my words.

"Yes, I'm taking myself out of this relationship, and I wish you the best of luck," I concluded with courage.

"Okay, if that's what you want, take care," was all he said. Carl was eating his dinner at the time, and had began to chew very slowly, as though he was in shock. Suddenly, the last supper, came to my mind. 'Was I acting as Judas did,' I wondered? betraying Jesus. Empty and lost, afraid of the unknown, I continued to follow my spiritual path with fear and trepidation.

CHAPTER 18

DISILLUSIONED

The next few days were hard. Disciplining myself from phoning Carl, was like starving my spirit of food. Although he was harsh with me, much of what Carl spoke was true. I needed to get a life, but how, I did not know. Desperate and unable to bear the pain without him, I weakened and phoned Carl once again.

On the other end of the phone, a female said, "you've got the wrong number," and hung up.

Unsure of what I had heard, I redialed the same number, the number I knew was Carl's. This time, he answered.

"A lady answered your phone. She said I had the wrong number." I was now anxious for his explanation.

"Oh take no notice of that. She just answered my phone and chose to say that, call me back in a minute and we'll have a chat," he said dismissively.

Feeling uneasy and scared, I prepared myself, rehearsing what I was going to say. I was now treading on new ground. The sound of thunder could me heard in the atmosphere. Taking in a deep breath, I slowly pressed the buttons on my phone; it was time to find out the truth. The truth of the matter. 'Who was this girl?' 'Was she his woman?' 'Was she the one that wanted his child?' 'Surely he couldn't have moved on already.'

Carl sounded really happy, like someone who'd just got married. In the background I could hear a lot of people laughing and joking. When he finally spoke to me properly, they all went silent, so I knew they were listening to our conversation.

"What do you want?" he asked rudely.

"Where are you?" I asked, clumsily.

"In McDonalds's with my brethren, and one woman of mine," he explained mockingly.

This surprised me, Carl always went on about the English food I ate, professing to be a vegetarian, and there he was in a burger bar.

Carl continued to mock me, so I hung up the phone, heartbroken and humiliated. I did not deserve this treatment. The man I thought was everything, a man of God with great wisdom, was treating me like an outcast. He showed no respect after all I'd done for him. All the giving, and the caring I had shown him, was dismissed in an instant. This was the ultimate insult. After everything I had been through in my life, Carl's final rejection, was to be the straw that broke the camels back. My mind, body, and soul, could not take in any more trauma and grief. My head felt as though it was about to split open with all the information it had absorbed over the years. I needed a release.

Looking at the two pictures of Carl at my bedside, with tears streaming down my face, I wanted to hurt him. I wanted him to feel what I was feeling. I had been abused for far too long. Thinking back, I remembered what an old neighbour had once done. She had stuck a pin in her boyfriend's private parts on a picture, because he had left her. When she next spoke to him, he told her, he had trouble in that area. It appeared to work.

As I poked the pin into Carl's eye, in the picture, I felt satisfied. Angry, I hoped he would go blind. That night I had a dream of myself looking in a mirror. Something was wrong with my eye. The next morning, I woke up, my eye felt sore. Looking in the mirror I had a large sty. It was the same eye as Carl's in the picture, which I had pricked. So it's an eye for an eye', I thought, realising I was now faced with a spiritual battle. I believed, whatever I did to Carl would happen to me. I could not go against the law of God!

Early one morning about eight, Carl phoned. Playing down my feelings, I coolly told him I was busy getting the children ready for school, and put the phone down. Carl persisted and phoned again later. To my delight, Carl was now chasing after me! My hopes of getting back with him were raised, but not for long. Carl stopped calling. Curiosity got the better of me, so I phoned him. This time to find out he was in bed with his girlfriend. He was just playing games with me.

"I can still speak to you, can't I," he insisted. How dare he? I still loved him. Didn't he know that?

Enraged, I resigned to the fact, Carl had no intention of getting back with me; I shouted my final words to him.

"Your nothing but a dirty bastard," I said, and hung up.

That night I could not sleep. I was gravely disturbed. An unbelievable fear surrounded me. I believed God was going to punish me, by throwing me into a lake of fire, for calling Carl such a horrible name. How could I get out of this? How could I put things right? The next morning, with lack of sleep, I made my way to Sandra's to find comfort. As I cried to her, telling her what I had done, she appeared uninterested.

"What you upset about? Is it because you didn't get your own way?" she questioned sarcastically, knowing full well I was longing to be back with him and how much I loved him. Her words gripped my heart.

As I sat there, in her presence, I dared not ask, why she was treating me this way.

"Anyway I have to go now. I'm going to London," Sandra continued, brushing my feelings aside. She was going to visit Carl's friend.

Trying to work out what I had done so wrong, I could not stop crying. The man I loved, had blocked me out of his life, and now my best friend was being cold towards me. No one seemed to love or care about me. Gathering my thoughts together, I went home, more lonely and lost than I had ever been in my life.

That night I had a dream of Carl speaking to Sandra. In the dream she looked up at me sheepishly. There was some kind of deception going on. But what?

Several days later Sandra came round to see me. She seemed humble and gentle, and said she had something to confess. She told me Carl's friend had asked about me.

"What did you say?" I was now excited that I was the interest of their conversation. I was in their thoughts.

"I told him what you said."

"Which was?"

"You said Carl slapped you on the cheek, and when you turned the other one, he slapped that too."

I had said that as a metaphor of how I'd been treated, and did not mind her telling him. Sandra went on to tell me that Carl's friend asked if I would go back out with Carl.

"What did you say?"

Feeling good again, I knew Carl in some way loved me, but wanted me to chase after him, as I had always done. However, this time I was tired... tired of doing all the giving. Sandra slowly raised her head and looked at me, with sheepish eyes, as she had in my dream. Speaking, counting her words, Sandra answered.

"Well... I...said...never."

My heart sank as her words swam around in my head. Sandra had seen me crying, knew how I felt, yet ruined all chances that were left for me with Carl. I was more in love than I had ever been before. This was no game.

I soon began to have flash backs.

'I'm surprise you're friends with her,' Oliver had said.

'You think she's your friend, but she's not. She slag's you off behind your back,' Nigel would say.

'Watch her,' Terence once said, when visiting the children. So many people had something to say. Why was she like this towards me? Only God knows the searing pain that I was feeling, in the depths of my heart. It was as though the control of my life had been snatched from me. Although I now know, it was God's plan to stop me from holding on to Carl.

Confiding in Beverly about what had happened, and what my ex-partners had said about Sandra, Beverly gave me her verdict.

"The majority rules," she stated, with great conviction. That was it. Her answer confirmed my fears, and fueled the hurt I was feeling.

The next day I was at the school waiting to pick my children up, when suddenly I felt completely overwhelmed, and could not breathe properly. I believed I was dying. Praying to God, to at least let me get home, with the children safely, I went across the playground, and sat on a bench. Hanging my head down, to see if that would help, Shekira suddenly appeared.

"I can't breathe," I told her.

I had to tell someone, just in case I did not make it home. The best person to tell was my child. Walking home slowly, my breathing gradually improved. I was not dying after all.

The next day I realised, I had to stay away from Sandra. She was damaging my health, as I blamed for everything. My hurt then went to rage. I always believed there was a process for bad news. First you go through hurt, anger, and then pain. I had been through the hurt, and was now going through the anger.

"Sandra stay away from me!" I screamed, as I heard her voice at the end of the telephone. "You've messed in my life with Oliver, and with Nigel, and now with Carl. Just stay away from me."

The ache in my heart felt like a sword had been pierced through it.

Turning to Beverly for reassurance, I told her what I'd done. She was the one who had given the verdict. I needed her comfort.

"He who is without sin let them cast the first stone," she quoted with hostility.

Not another one, I thought. What had I done to her? I had forgiven her for the past, and now she appeared to be playing games with my mind. No one seemed to care about me. I was so desperate to be loved and to be noticed.

Isolated and lonely, with my back against the wall with no-one to help me, my mind crashed, like an overloaded computer. It could not cope with any more data and viruses. Everything that had been entered had to be wiped out, before the reprogramming of my mind could begin.

My immunity against violence, mental abuse, and rejection, had broken down. I did not know who I was any more, and suffered a mental breakdown. All the pains and anguishes, I'd hidden in the past, came to the surface. The times, when I could not express myself, and had to repress my feelings. The inadequacies and worthlessness, that was projected by others onto me, making me feel as though I was a nobody. These thoughts were out of my control. There was nothing I could do about it, but let it happen. The different scenes of my life flashed in and out of my conscious state. It was excruciating. I felt as though I needed a large amount valium, injected into my veins. I wished my heart could be taken out of my body. To get rid of the pain.

In the midst of this turmoil, my spirit convinced me to put my trust in God, knowing that he could help me. It would only be a matter of time, until I would feel better. I became a walking zombie. I could not eat or sleep and could not tell anyone what I was experiencing. I believed, I knew what they would say. 'It's Fiona again.' I couldn't take the risk, so I took Rueben to one side, and told him that he would have to run the house for a week. He would have to cook and look after his sisters, to give me time and space to get well. It would take just one more thing to happen, and I would never recover or be the same again. There would be no more Fiona.

I read through psalms and prayed and begged God with all my heart and soul to help me. I took no tablets to help because I did not want to numb what I was feeling, otherwise I would never know whether I was getting better or not. I just wanted everything to come out.

Coming to the understanding, of what the saying meant, 'there is a very thin line between sanity and insanity,' I chose sanity. To have this, is a precious thing. So I waited patiently and humbly, for God to show me what to do next.

After a week, I left the house for the first time and visited Diane, and I told her of my recent happenings.

"Someone's looking after you, look at all the things you've been through yet you're still here."

I knew what Diane meant. Someone above was protecting me. I believed God had placed an angel over me. I always seemed to get through.

Knowing I would never be let down by God, I continued on my spiritual journey, fragile and weak. To re-program my mind I had to break the pattern of abuse, by identifying where the origin of abuse came from. If an incident hasn't been dealt with in the first place, it will happen again and again until it is. There were four issues I had to deal with;

Firstly, where did the acceptance of violence come from, and how did I see it as a form of love? I identified, that it arose from my childhood. Although I knew my mother loved me very much, she used to discipline me quite harshly, to keep me under control. Being strict as a parent was normal in those times. Subconsciously I believed, when my partners used violence as a form of control over me, they really loved me. Even though on asking Nigel why he treated me the way he did, he told me, it was because he was jealous of me. Nevertheless, it was the concept of how I saw the meaning of love that needed to change. Love is not cruel, it is kind.

Secondly, why did I always do as I was told to please everyone? As a child, I was always obedient, and wanted to please my mum. I would do anything that she asked or told me to do without complaining. This behaviour was a part of my character as an adult. I never said no. This was not a good thing as I would always put other people's needs first, before mine and my children's.

Thirdly, why did people, such as friends, family, and boyfriends, treat me like a child? I had not matured and did not behave like an adult. I was treated according to my childlike ways. 'You're cute,' was a statement people often made until I became sick of it. I wanted them to see me as a person, and not a toy. The suppression I suffered in my relationships, had built on my quiet natured personality over the years. Instead of developing and growing into the person I should be, my growth was stunted.

Fourthly, why didn't I speak up immediately when someone offended me? And if, on the rare occasions when I did, why did I get nasty? I felt this was the only way I could be heard. In my early years, being angry, would get my message across, especially if I felt people were walking all over me. This worked for me as an adult, although this was the wrong way to respond.

I felt it was my own fault for allowing everything to happen to me. I now had to find an even balance in my personality and life. But most of all, I had to grow up! The only way to do this was to break the cycle of abuse, and to find out who I was.

I had to go back into the past to when friends had originally failed me. The pattern had to be broken, to enable myself to be healed. No matter how hard I had tried to be nice, or just be myself, there was always something coming up against me. I had to finally put a stop to it.

Writing everything down that I felt on a daily basis, helped to release the pressure of my thoughts and feelings as God took me back to the formation of my life. The mysteries of my life were soon understood, and I could see things about myself clearer. My mind could now be re-programmed, so that I could start my life again. This time, replacing the impressions of the world, with the impressions of God.

CHAPTER 19

SEARCHING FOR THE TRUTH

Several weeks had passed and I was still in distress about Carl. I had not heard from him, and felt everyone had moved on, and I was left behind, all on my own. The only hope and comfort I had were in the dreams and visions, God had given, to guide me in this time of need. All I could say to myself was 'the harder the battle, the sweeter the victory'. Time would heal my brokenness.

As part of my healing process, in spite of all that had gone on, God sent me to forgive Sandra, to say sorry for how I had spoken to her. I was in emotional bondage because of my confrontation with her, and needed to be set free. And, I needed answers. Fearfully I went to see her.

Sandra coldly let me in. I explained how sorry I was for the way I had spoken to her, and asked her why she had treated me the way she did. Raising her voice she responded abruptly.

"Sorry... for anything I've done to you, but I don't care. I stand in the line of correction."

Meaning God would discipline her and forgive her. She showed no remorse or love towards me. She just did not care. Feeling dismayed, I walked away. I had done my bit for the sake of God. I could do no more.

Late one night, in the winter months, my life took a new turn. I had run out of electricity and needed to get to the nearest garage which sold electric cards. Natasha was the only port of help nearby. She had a car; I didn't and could not drive.

"Can you take me to get some electric?" I asked.

"No, I'm tired," she said. "I'm half asleep in bed. I'll baby-sit while you go," she added.

'Why is she being like this?' I thought. I was already in enough pain. Upset, I started to cry, taking her response personally. So Natasha phoned mum and dad, who came quickly to my aid. I couldn't appreciate, she was tired. She had worked hard all day, and had to look after her own children.

"You're a walking fool," mum told me whilst I was in the back of her car screaming. "You shouldn't keep saying yes to everyone, and when you want them to do something for you, expect them to do it. Maybe it's not convenient for them, to do what you want. You can say no too."

My dad joined in and explained to me how irresponsible I was. He said I should make sure that I had the necessary resources for myself and the children, by planning ahead and not waiting until the last minute to provide.

Although I felt rejected for the umpteenth time, I knew what mum and day was saying, was right. Just because I would feel obliged to do what people asked of me, it did not mean that everyone else felt the same. If they had things to do, or were in a position to help, they would not hesitate to say yes or no. So why couldn't I. Natasha was exhausted. She later explained that if she had driven her car whilst in that state, she might have had an accident. I wished I could be like her, and be honest with myself. Unfortunately I would agree to everything, causing myself to fall. Like the times I would take Troy and Nigel back, knowing they would cause me pain. And the times when I would give Carl money because he said he needed it, leaving me, and the children without. I just could not find it within myself, to ever say no.

"Start saying no to people, and start buying things for yourself and your home bit by bit," mum advised. "You'll soon see how everything accumulates."

Taking on mum's advice, I carefully restructured my finances. Every time I had any money, before leaving my house, I would pray and ask God to bless it, and spend it for me. An idea I had got from Sandra. Eventually a year later I had everything I needed. My life with my children became more in order as they began to respect me for meeting their needs for once, and not always the needs of others!

During this time, God lead me through the Old Testament of the bible, step by step. He wanted to show me something. I had to find out the truth about Rasta and God for myself. Whilst searching the scriptures, many things came to light. As a result, I concluded, that to remove any guilt from sin, the offering of an unblemished lamb would be used as a sacrifice to God for cleansing purposes. To cleanse us of all our unrighteousness. The lamb would be killed, and its blood would be sprinkled at the altar in the Lords temple. The Holy of Holies. God's dwelling place. Only a high priest, who wore special clothing, and no one else, could take the blood into this place, on behalf of Gods people. Because I wanted to do things right I became desperate to take part in this. Even though I was still unsure of what sins I had, I wanted to do what God expected of me. I needed to be included in the ceremony of the blood sacrifice, so that I could be cleansed. So off I went to see Beverly again for advice.

"Why don't Rasta's carry out the rituals in the Old Testament, since that's what they believe in?" I asked.

"Because you can't perform those duties in England, it would be impossible," she explained.

Beverly's explanation seemed justifiable to me. I imagined someone doing this sacrifice. They would probably be arrested, or be seen as a mentally disturbed person. Regardless, I believed we still needed to do this. It was God's requirement.

Continuing my research, my eating habits changed. The covenant stated that you must not eat certain meats. This gave me an understanding of why meat eating Rasta's, did not eat certain meats, such as pork. It was regarded as unclean. Taking in what I had read, like the majority of

Rasta's, I became a vegetarian. I cooked only fish and vegetables for myself and the children. But this did not last long. I craved meat!

Within the law, there were other symbolic things you had to do. For example: If you had a dreaded skin disease you would not comb your hair. To me, this contradicted the reason, why as a Rasta, you should not comb your hair.

The more I read the bible, the more things did not fit into place. I could not find any mention of being a Rasta in the bible. I so wanted to get things right. My quest for the truth was far from over.

The deeper I got into my search, the more I became fearful of doing something wrong, if I did not do everything according to the bible, and live up to the expectations of God. Because of the heavy presence surrounding me, which I had invited in, I thought God was horrible. Carrying on, determined, I continued my studies.

The popular story of Noah's ark, which I knew from Sunday school, was emphasised to me. Understanding the power in the story, it showed that God, if he wanted to, could wipe out all of creation, saving only those who were seen as righteous. Also if He says He is going to do something, He does. Terrified and worried that I might not be saved from God's wrath at the end times, I was determined to stay away from anyone that might cause me to fall.

On my search, to discover more about Rastafarianism, I began to read up about Africa and Haile Selassie. Since I could not find his name in the bible, I wanted to know what the connection was between the bible, Africa and Haile Selassie.

I first discovered that in Africa, there were different tribes of people, each tribe having its own name. This was the same with Carl's movement and with Beverly's. Both had tribal names. Carl's movement had names similar to the African tribes, whereas Beverly's, 'twelve tribes of Israel', came from the bible. Everything seemed mixed up.

In reading about Haile Selassie, I found he was born of Christian descent. Because of this, I came to believe that he was the next stage from Jesus, of the manifestation of God.

Focusing on this thought, I also began to relate to the Israelites. God's chosen people in the bible, who were also once slaves. Confirming my belief, I was one of God's people, because I was different, just like them. I did wonder, where white people fitted into God's realm. Since all blacks and Jews were God's children, what about other nationalities? Surely, we must all come from the same place. If there was only one God, wouldn't He be the God of all nations, and why did He make us all different?

Finding the answer to my concern in the bible, where it stated that the whole earth was of one nation, satisfied me. God saw that because men had one language and were one nation, they were capable of doing what they wanted, without His permission. Men had thought they were clever, and decided to make bricks, and build a city, and a tower, that may reach heaven. The tower of Babel. So He mixed up our languages so we could not understand one another, and scattered us around the face of the earth. It appeared to make sense, we did have the same God and that each nation worshipped God in their own way, calling him a different name.

This belief was confirmed by Beverly. She said there were different rooms in Gods house, and she was making sure she was going in the room with the Rasta's. A room I was heading for, but not really wanting to go into. It seemed dark and gloomy. And I did not want to keep up with the rituals. It was impossible for me. I would still be in bondage. Besides, why would God want to separate us nations into different rooms? To me this was saying that we would still be separated in heaven, just like here on earth.

I then read about Joseph, and his dream about the sun, moon and the stars. The sun and moon represented his mother and father, and the stars his brothers. I began to relate to this as the source of the idea that Haile Selassie represented the sun and Princess Menen represented the moon. The stars were the Rasta's. God's children.

I found it was also wrong to call upon the spirits of the dead, sorcery, divination, anything spiritualist. I was still fascinated with talking about the spirit realm with Diane, but the scriptures made it clear that the things I was relying on for comfort and direction were not of God. They were false spirits, deceiving us to draw us away from believing in God. I stopped immediately. The card readings, belief in horoscopes, oracles and believing in mediums and spirits speaking to me. Again wanting to please God.

I found King David and King Solomon were Kings from the tribe Judah. Although Carl had said Haile Selassie was a descendent of King David, I could not find any information on this. In regards to King Solomon, he did have many wives and many mistresses. This was against the law of God, which said we shouldn't commit adultery. Yet Carl had used King Solomon, as a justification to carry out his abuse.

Idolatry appeared to be a main issue. The Israelites sinned against God, making their own images of Him out of gold and clay, which they worshipped. I questioned whether I was guilty of this, as I had an image of God on a photograph and in my mind. Not sure, I tried my hardest not to focus on the image I had, but on the spirit.

Psalms and Proverbs continued to be of encouragement, especially in my time of loneliness and solitude, together with the book of Job. Job's faith was tested by God. God let his adversary take away all he possessed including his family leaving him with nothing. That was exactly how I felt. I had lost all my friends and family. Job eventually was blessed by God with more than he originally had. This book gave me another hope. I thought maybe God was testing my faith. Persevering, I continued my search, drawn to what God was yet to show me.

The Old Testament was all I read. I never looked at the New Testament in my Bible as I saw it as a separate book. The only part I did read, was the book of Revelation as it mentioned 'The King of Kings' and 'The rider on the white horse.' The things Carl had imprinted in my mind about Haile Selassie. But my main confusion still stood. If Rasta was God's path, and we were supposed to obey the written laws, as in the Old Testament, how was I going to carry them out?

As time went on, I became defensive about my new found faith, which had become my security. For once, I had my own identity, so whenever anyone said anything negative about it, I would react angrily. A friend once said,

"I used to believe in Haile Selassie, until I found out what he was like. He mistreated the poor and gave all the food to the lions, leaving the people hungry."

Angry I defended my belief.

"Well if we don't do as we're told, then God will punish us," I told him, deciding not to see him again. No one, was going to take away what I had.

Sitting on my settee one afternoon, lonely and sad, not knowing where I was heading in life, I heard a strong firm voice in an audible manner. It was a voice that no man can imitate. It was soft and gentle but with strength behind it. I am not sure whether I was in a trance when this happened or fully awake. All I know is I was not conscious of my surroundings.

"You have been given the seal of approval," the voice told me.

Appearing in front of me was a big hand, holding a seal. The hand moved towards me, and stamped the seal on my forehead. I felt real peace. In the vision, I could see other people. They were queuing up, waiting, to see God to receive their reward. God was kind. He was not all dark and gloomy in the way I had perceived him to be, waiting to punish me for every wrong move. The heavy presence, I was feeling around me, was different from the peace I had just felt.

Unexpectedly, the book of Revelation came to mind. Fear gripped me again. Had I received the mark of the beast on my forehead. The mark, which the Rasta friends of my teenage years had told me about? As I searched, in the book of Revelation I found a scripture in chapter 7 verse 3. It affirmed, the seal of approval. It read, 'Do not harm the land or the sea or the trees until we put a seal on the foreheads of the servants of our God.' I was exalted. I was chosen. God approved of me. Me, Fiona, of all people. Societies reject… The person that no one noticed. It was the greatest thing that had happened to me. This kept me going as I knew for sure, I was chosen. Special in the eyes of God. But what was this darkness? Spiritually something in the atmosphere was making me feel scared, and physically sick. This presence, which I had always thought was God, was now open to my questioning. Making me doubt, whether what I had been worshipping, was in fact God.

I then had a dream of needles and thread. In the dream was a group of white people sitting in a circle. A lady stood up and spoke. 'Now for your next lesson in life,' she said. I interpreted this to mean, God was going take me to the next level of my journey. My life was going to be sewn back together again.

Shortly after this dream, Diane's dad died, who was my uncle. She informed me that there was a bible of mine at his house. I knew this was part of the next step of my spiritual journey. As she handed it over to me, I noticed it was the New Testament only. The part of the bible I hadn't read.

"How do you know its mine?" I asked curiously.

"Look inside; it's got your name in it."

I opened it and read, 'Fiona lynch'. It was my hand writing. It was given to me at school when I was eleven years old, and now it was in my hands. At the right time!

As I started to read the New Testament, the mystery of my dreams began to unfold. All the damaged and torn things, of the past began to come up. Everything needed sewing back together again. This started to happen when Sarah approached me, to tell me about a Christian group, named 'Focus,' she was setting up in her house. It was for those who were feeling lost, and needed sanctuary. The group sounded like a good idea. Anything was worth a try. Even though I believed I had found God, I was dying inside. I felt as though I was walking through the valley of death spiritually; feeling all sorts of bitterness, resentment and all sorts of ill-feelings. My 'next lesson in life' was to be found in this group. There was something I needed to know, and something I needed to learn.

My first visit to the group was good. I was the only black person there, but felt comfortable and safe away from my own culture. Maggie was at the group. She had her own issues too, which helped me. I was not the only one. She said God had told her to shake my hand when she first met me, and said I was going to be her boss in the future. I could not see how that could be. I was not capable of doing anything.

Feeling loved for once, I couldn't wait to go every Tuesday evening without fail. Different subjects were taught from the New Testament. I'd go and often, the talk would be on the same subject that I had been led to read that week. Such as, anger, pain, anxiety, hurt, and forgiveness, and what God says about them all. We would then pray about these issues, giving them over to God. I began to feel alive again. One time I had severe back pain; a young lady and a young man, layed their hands on me and prayed in Jesus' name. The pain went. I could see something different about them. There faces shone, and they were full of love. One guy stood out. Although he was young, he had devoted his life to Jesus. Once I watched whilst he prayed. I could see he had a personal relationship with God. I wanted the same. Even though I had my beliefs, I did not feel connected to God.

Sarah gave me a lot of attention. She would take me food shopping, and out for lunch. I could knock on her and Maggie's door at any time of the day, and they would welcome me with open arms. Sometimes even early in the morning or late at night. Going to the group and reading the New Testament, opened up many questions that could now be answered.

My earlier experiences of taking abuse from friends were now in front of me. I needed healing. The root problem of each relationship, over the years needed addressing. I needed to allow new seeds to be sewn in my heart, to enable me to grow in the right way. I needed to change my character. I needed to let people know straight away if they offended me, rather than hide it away. By storing things up, and adding negative emotions into my heart and mind, I was causing hurt to myself and to others.

Beverly had let me down at the beginning of my life's journey, and had got into the habit of treating me a certain way. I did not speak up to her when she first offended me, by setting me up with Hubert. So she continued to treat me in the same way, as an adult. Always careless about my feelings, because of her perception of me, and because she believed she could. It appeared, I accepted whatever she did to me or said, by not complaining.

I believed Sandra caused trouble where my boyfriends were concerned, because of what had happened between Oliver and I. She was used to having a friendship with them, as though it was okay, as I had never confronted her about Oliver. I just took it.

I had become a lost cause to my family and friends because I had chosen to walk on a path of destruction. I had shut them out. It was my responsibility to help myself. Not theirs. I did not know who I was, and there were no real changes throughout my life. How could I expect anyone to treat me in the way I wanted?

By identifying these issues, bringing them to the group, I was able to get prayers for healing in these areas. I had to break the pattern, by changing my victim mindset, and allow my self to mature. This was going to be a hard process.

I really enjoyed the group, but in my confusion, I still believed that Haile Selassie was God. I hoped someday soon, I could mention this to them, to tell them that they hadn't quite got the truth. Haile Selassie was the Almighty God, the next manifestation of Jesus. Although they were helping me, I became worried about following their Christian beliefs about Jesus, so I stopped going, and continued to worship Haile Selassie as my God.

Alone again, I found it difficult to connect to God. The darkness appeared to be looming above my head and around me, more and more. Ready to punish me if I made the wrong move. Isolating myself, I only left the house if I had too.

"Why don't you come back to the group?" asked Sarah's daughter, who dared to visit me. They were concerned as they had not seen me for a while.

"I'm scared of getting contaminated," I told her.

"Why would you get contaminated?" she asked.

"If I mix, I might do the wrong things. All I want to do is please God."

"But you've got everything going for you. You've built up your house, and you've now got everything in order. Go out there and live life," she encouraged. But I did not want to. The spirit that with me, was keeping me from socialising, because of the hold it had over me. It had taken total control of my life, and I was afraid of losing my sanity.

"Just come back one more time and see. I will leave you alone after that," she promised.

Agreeing to her offer, I returned to the group. I was alarmed when they sang a song claiming Jesus was God of all. That night, at home, I remember feeling as though I was being strangled. The two different spirits were entangling me. I wanted the spirit of Jesus away from me. I thought it was Jesus doing this to me. As far as I was concerned Haile Selassie was the earth's rightful ruler, and no-one could say I was wrong. Distressed, I stayed away from everyone in the group again.

During my time of solitude, a picture appeared in my mind. Putting pencil to paper, I drew the image I could see. There was a river running down the middle of a city. On each side of the river was a fruit tree. I later found I had drawn the river of life referred to in the bible. It was about God's city where He would live with us, and the trees were for the healing of the nations. But how do I enter this city?

At this time I had another dream. In the dream were two boys. One was black and the other white. God was looking down. I interpreted that, in God's city, there is no segregation. Blacks and whites lived together.

As I became more interested in what the bible said, Beverly began to change even more towards me. I still needed some answers from her, so would occasionally visit her. But it was as though she was shutting the door, to what I thought was God's Kingdom in my face.

"What about the Holy Spirit?" I asked her. "I'm trying to get filled with it."

Beverly threw her head back and laughed at me.

"What!" she exclaimed, as though I was mad.

Her response contradicted what she had said before, no one should remove anything from the Bible. Yet this was what she, was doing.

After ridiculing me, Beverly slipped up by letting me know she had been mixing with Sandra behind my back. She had obviously been reporting to Sandra, everything I had shared with her. She had been deceiving me all along. Slowly, drifting away from her, I made a decision. I would never let her, or anyone else, walk all over me, again.

CHAPTER 20

FINDING THE TRUTH

Leaving everyone to their own devices, the reality of everything became clearer. Something in my heart was telling me, I hadn't quite got the truth. It was as though I was given a photographic memory by God, revealing snapshots that my mind had taken throughout my relationship with Carl. These snapshots became my guide. I realised some of the things Carl had said to me, were what Jesus says in the bible. Picturing Carl, I remembered when he had said, we must 'love one another,' and that 'love was the greatest gift' he could offer me. God had obviously been speaking to me, through Carl. Without love, I concluded, we would always be hurting each other. With love we would try our hardest to do the right thing. Each piece of information was like a piece of a jigsaw puzzle to the mystery trail.

As I continued to study the New Testament, I began to examine myself, and my behaviour towards others. I found, I had sins too, and that nobody's perfect. I was busy blaming others for my downfalls, and judging them for their ways, using them as 'the scapegoat' for my downfalls in life. I had been horrible to people myself. People had issues too. I needed to be aware of this. What I needed to do was recognise if someone was unhealthy for me, to avoid them.

Proceeding with my search, I was given the image of Carl on our second meeting. It seemed as if he was solid, like a stone. There was a spiritual feeling to this stone. Had I rejected the important person in building my life? I felt as though I had, since I discarded him. I questioned whether seeing the words 'the Almighty,' and a voice saying 'do it now,' was just my imagination.

Another day on waking, the word 'scepter' appeared. It was as if it was in my hand. I remembered when I first met Carl, and he spoke about princes and princesses, and how he appeared like royalty to me. But something was not quite right. I was still being led to something else, the person who held the royal scepter.

I was still very lonely and felt strongly led to go back to 'Focus,' where I was welcomed with open arms. I joined in with their worship singing; Jesus is Lord. This time I felt more at peace with myself, and did not feel strangled. After having more pictures and images, many other things were confirmed.

"You are a sheep among wolves," Sarah said once, after praying with me.

What Sarah did not know was I had previously seen a vision of wolves coming after me. I had questioned whether Carl and the people I had been mixing with were the wolves. Pretending to be someone that they're not.

I read about false teachers who exploit those who were still vulnerable. Those trying to walk away from the mistakes, they had made in their lives. When I met Carl I was trying to walk away from a bad life with Nigel. A life that was so wrong. I was vulnerable, and I hadn't found stability yet. I would lean on anyone that showed me attention. Although he taught me some good things, Carl also took advantage of me, and used his faith to control me.

As God took me backwards again to the beginning of my time on earth, I discovered the depth of my sins, and where they came from. For example, why did I smoke, and take drugs. God showed me it was easy for me to do, because the idea was planted in my mind when I was a child. Then I remembered, when I heard my mum saying, my uncle, who smoked weed, had got into trouble, and was locked up for having drugs in his house.

Also, why did I swear so much? The people in my culture swore a lot. It was normal. Every other word was a swear word. As I came to the beginning of my life on earth, I had the sensation, of when I saw myself in a pram, and I felt as though I was somewhere looking down. I believed I was where God was. In front of me above the world, was a city. A new one. I could see the outline of it. I could now see the world from a spiritual point of view. The game monopoly came to mind. Life was like this game, a game of gain; properties and businesses, a game that I did not know how to play. I had become stagnated and incapable. To play this game, I had to finish my spiritual course, then I could start my life again. God had more to reveal. The time was coming to find the key. The key to the hidden treasures that I thought I had found in Rastafarianism.

"Haile Selassie said do not call me God," I remembered Beverly telling me. Yet everyone called him this, including Beverly and myself. If Haile Selassie said this, then who is God? In my confusion I continued my search.

"When I worship I feel like there's nothing around me," I confided one day to Sarah.

"Oh do yah, like your flapping in air? The bible talks about the prince of the air," she told me.

Sarah words struck me. It was exactly how I felt. She always seemed to know what I was going through. She said before she became a Christian, she was a witch. She had experienced many spiritual situations. So was familiar with some of the things I would say. I became more interested in 'Focus,' and began to listen more and more on the teachings of Jesus. I would receive great encouragement from everyone, especially Maggie. She would sit with me and make me laugh.

One evening, Sarah taught on the subject of judgment. I was scared. I did not want to displease God in case I went to hell, a place without love, a place I felt I had been all my life. Those who did not believe that Jesus was the son of God would be cast out on the Day of Judgment. The fear was not the same as I had felt, before I was baptized years ago.

Even though they had taught something similar, this was different. I had come to know that God meant love not condemnation. Hell was a place where I would be separated from this love. I wanted that love.

That night I read the first part of the first chapter in the book of John. The mystery of the scripture was revealed to me. The revelation of who Jesus was became clear. Jesus was God. He has always existed.

The next day whilst strolling back from the shop, the dream I had of the light-bulb came true. It happened all of a sudden when the spirit of Jesus fell upon me. I can remember having an overwhelming sense of peace as my heart testified, 'Jesus is the Christ.' Looking up at the sky, His Spirit appeared to fill the whole universe. I felt like someone had switched a light on inside my mind. As the light of Jesus shone from within, I could now see. All darkness was gone. I could see the spirit I had been worshipping of Haile Selassie, as a minute particle in the air. The revelation was so clear. There were no doubts any more. Jesus, was the Key I was looking for. The key to eternal life, and to the hidden treasures. He is the one and only creator of the universe.

The scriptures I had been reading became clearer as God revealed the truth to me. Jesus was the King the prophets had spoken about who was coming, to bring salvation to man. The book of Isaiah chapter 7 verse 14, was one such confirmation. Therefore the Lord himself will give a sign: The virgin will be with child and will birth a son, and will call him Immanuel,' meaning, 'God with us'. Mary conceived as a virgin and gave birth to Jesus. I could see how Jesus when on earth was God in the flesh. He had become the sacrificial lamb by dying on the cross to take away our guilt from sin and to save us from eternal death through the shedding of his blood. No more rituals. The old Law and covenant no longer exists. Our bodies are now the temple of God. We do not need to go into a building, the tabernacle, where the spirit of God would have been. God now lives in us, if we invite him in. He is the high priest. We don't need anyone to go into the Holy of Holies for us, we can enter ourselves, through Jesus.

Reaching home, I realised that Jesus was the Conquering Lion of the Tribe of Judah spoken of in the book of Revelation. He conquered all evil, temptation and deceit in the world. He held the royal scepter. He was the coming king, from the line of King David. He is the King of Kings and Lord of Lords.

As my eyes became more and more opened, I could now see that my UFO experiences were just an illusion performed by the enemy to draw me away from God. In addition, I was deceived in believing that Haile Selassie was God, because of the colour of my skin, and my position in society as a black person.

Everything in the New Testament was in a spiritual context. Instead of living under the obedience of the law written on stone as in the Old Testament, it was now to be written on hearts through the Spirit of Jesus, so that we can live a life in the spirit rather than in the flesh.

It was a Sunday afternoon when a strange feeling came over me. Now that I had found the truth, I felt I had to make a decision. To either continue in my darkness or accept the light. The spirit I had been worshiping was still with me. Although I had the revelation of who Jesus was, I was still in bondage. I just wanted this dark spirit to go away. With great urgency, I became desperate to be baptized. I now knew what this meant. I needed to get rid of all the past. Have it all washed away. I wanted to die with Christ, and rise with Christ into His resurrection. I could hear the words, 'go and be baptized in the name of the father and of the son and of the Holy Ghost.' At that precise moment, there was a knock at the door. It was Sarah. Her timing was right. She had not known anything about what I had just experienced.

"Erm, have you been baptized?" she asked warily as though she was treading on ice.

Feeling embarrassed, as she had been right about Jesus all along, I snapped back defensively with pride.

"Yes, when I was nineteen."

"Oh, I just thought I'd ask, I've been baptized before, but I'm doing it again, as a reaffirmation of my faith."

Sarah left and said she would let me know the date of her baptism.

Going over my life, I felt greatly convicted by God. All my sins were exposed. The things that I had forgotten I had done, were now in the forefront of my mind. I had been totally disobedient to God. I lived a life doing my own will, to my destruction. I had behaved against God's plans for my life, causing myself pain. I had failed myself and others. Mainly my children.

The shame of how I had lived, the squalor, the drugs, the abuse, the foul language, were now staring me in the face. I wished I could hide from myself. I felt unclean. I just wanted this embarrassment to go away when a white piece of paper appeared in front of me. It had nothing written on it. 'My sins have been forgiven through 'The Holy Trinity', Haile Selassie, Bob Marley and Marcus Garvey,' I could hear Carl's words in my mind. These three were the opposite of the Christian believe of the Godhead; the Father the Son and the Holy Ghost. Repentance came to mind. I needed to turn away from my sins. Be cleansed and have a clean sheet.

Going to 'Focus' on the Tuesday, I wanted to know what I had to do to follow Jesus, and have my sins forgiven.

"You have to do a prayer." Sarah told me. "You need to repent and give everything over to the cross of Jesus Christ," she continued.

"Let's do it now," I responded, with great urgency. Remembering psalm 118, which Carl had read to me saying, 'The stone which the builders had rejected as worthless has become the headstone of the corner,' I realised this stone was Jesus. In building my life, I had rejected the most important stone. The cornerstone. I needed to rebuild my life with this stone in place. I had put my trust in people and not in God.

Crumbled and crushed I repeated the prayer as Sarah spoke.

"Dear Lord Jesus, I'm sorry for the things I've done. I believe that you are the Christ, and invite you into my life as my Lord and saviour."

Resting my head on Sarah's shoulder, floods of tears just poured and poured down my face, as the bondage of hurt, pain and rejection from the beatings and abuse that had been dealt to me in my life, were broken. In place was the love of God. I was finally free from my oppression. I could now walk freely in the light of Jesus Christ. I had crossed over, 'from darkness to light.'

About a week later, Sarah came round with a scripture from her bible.

"God has prompted me to give you this reading, but I don't know what it means, but I think you will."

The reading was from Jeremiah chapter 7. It talked about the queen of heaven. This scripture confirmed what I had been taught by Carl and Sandra was wrong. On further reading chapter 44, Jeremiah continues to talk about worshipping the Queen of heaven as idolatry. In addition, in Deuteronomy chapter 17 verses 2 to 5, declares that anyone found worshipping the sun, the moon, and any host in heaven, should be stoned until they die. I was blind when reading the scriptures, but now I could see. There is one God and one route to reconciliation with God, not several.

I had sought all the ways of the spiritual world for answers to life, but none could give them to me. Although some things, like some of the oracles, the mediums, and what my gypsy friend had said came true, the source of the information was not from God. He used them to bring me back to Him. My gypsy friend has since confessed this to me, and told me how it all started for her. She has now stopped reading palms, and telling fortunes, as she believes it is wrong in the sight of God. The spiritual activities that were not Godly that surrounded my life, the tarot cards, the horoscopes and spiritual books, were all part of my journey. None brought me happiness only frustration. Amongst them all, God spoke to me, through my dreams and visions.

The next stage of my salvation was to be baptized. Walk in a new creation, and take on Gods name. The words 'blessed is he that comes in the name of the Lord,' plagued my mind. I could not understand what this meant, until I bumped into a woman that I had known in the past. She was a born again Christian. She explained to bury with Christ, and to rise with Christ into his resurrection, I had to be baptized in Jesus' name, by full immersion in water. By going down into the water I was burying my past, and rising out, to be a new person. Everything would be washed away, never to haunt me again. She gave details from the scriptures about the Godhead, which many called the Trinity. She said the common name of the Father and of the Son and of the Holy Spirit was Jesus. There is not three God's but one. God operates in these roles for redemption purposes.

He came as a son, to be equal with us, and that the Holy Spirit was His spirit. This made perfect sense to me as she continued to show me that the disciples baptized many in Jesus name.

My baptism was an amazing experience. As soon as I came out of the water, I felt clean. I had entered God's kingdom. My past life was now washed away, and I had become re-born in Christ. A spiritual birth. A weight had lifted from my soul, and I felt new. I now belonged to God. I knew He loved me, for who I was to eternity.

EPILOGUE

THE HIDDEN TREASURES

Since my conversion, I have continued to walk in the will of God for my life, by following Jesus. I found that the hidden treasures were the gifts of wisdom and knowledge, which is needed to be successful in this life, and the gifts and talents within me, which Jesus the key, has unlocked.

At present I am the Pastor of 'The Church of United Nations,' in Cambridge, England. My character and life has changed so much. The past has no hold over me. As soon as I gave my life to Jesus, many doors were opened. I have had many good job opportunities. I have written this book, and bible courses, and am in the process of writing others. I can now drive, which is useful in my ministry. I am always in the process of doing something new. I had never travelled far before, especially on my own, until I went to Guyana, where I was ordained. Whilst there, I preached the gospel at several churches. Speaking in public was something that I would never even have dreamt of before. I can now speak up with confidence in any situation.

My children are a blessing to me. I am now able to provide them with a better quality of life. God has taught me, what it means to be a parent. We now have friendship, communication, love, and I am immensely proud of them.

Despite the trials and tribulations of life, I know that God will always be there to help me through. I try not to look too far ahead, as I have found, I could make all the plans in the world, but God has the last say. He is control. His plans for me have been far greater, than what I had ever anticipated for myself.